Especia [barcode]

D0288759

....

From

....

Date

....

ANITA HIGMAN & MARIAN LESLIE

3-MINUTE
PRAYERS
for Moms

BARBOUR BOOKS
An Imprint of Barbour Publishing, Inc.

© 2018 by Barbour Publishing, Inc.

ISBN 978-1-68322-417-4

Published by Barbour Books, an imprint of Barbour Publishing, Inc., 1810 Barbour Drive, Uhrichsville, Ohio 44683, www.barbourbooks.com

Our mission is to inspire the world with the life-changing message of the Bible.

Member of the
Evangelical Christian
Publishers Association

Printed in the United States of America.

INTRODUCTION

Watching your kids grow up is by far one of the most exhilarating, awe-inspiring, petrifying passages of a lifetime! The only way to make it through this merry gauntlet is to cling to the Lord Jesus with all your might. Here is a collection of prayers with reflections to get you started along your journey—and that divine clinging—to the Master Artist, who designed every miraculous part of your child, right down to that irresistible giggle.

God is right here, right now. And He's waiting to hear from you. . . .

YOUR LOVING EYE ON ME!

*I will instruct you and teach you in
the way you should go; I will counsel
you with my loving eye on you.*

PSALM 32:8

Okay, I admit it, Lord. Some days I like to think of
myself as a super mom. I can almost imagine my
back bolt straight, my hands on my hips, and my
cape unfurling in the breeze. And at that moment,
I'm certain people are whispering, "It's a bird. It's
a plane. It's Super Mom!" Then on other days—like
today—I realize no one would dare think I deserved
a recycled Mother's Day card! I don't know what
I'm doing. I need Your help and guidance. Not
just on days when I'm panic-ridden and clueless,
but every day, Lord. I need Your loving eye on me,
Your teachable moments directed at me, and Your
divine roadmap spread before me! Amen.

THINK ABOUT IT:
Why do you pull away from God and His
guidance—sometimes even when you need Him
most?

WHATEVER IS LOVELY

Finally, brothers and sisters, whatever is true, whatever is noble, whatever is right, whatever is pure, whatever is lovely, whatever is admirable— if anything is excellent or praiseworthy— think about such things.

PHILIPPIANS 4:8

Oh Lord, our family is bombarded with the world's mess, and it seems to get uglier every week. We're blasted with meanness, violence, lies, bullying, greed, foul language, bigotry, and shocking lewdness everywhere we turn. It comes from TV shows, movies, the news, out on the street, school buses, stores, commercials, magazines, computer games, and social media. We can't always get away from it. Jesus, please protect my family members from these fearsome attacks that keep us from thinking on whatever is good, lovely, and noble. Amen.

THINK ABOUT IT:
What are some practical things God is prompting you to do to limit the world's negative influence on you and your family?

THAT URGING IN MY SOUL

*"Blessed are the peacemakers, for they
will be called children of God."*

MATTHEW 5:9

Holy Spirit, I guess You've noticed—painfully so—that I can be a petty person. I sometimes bicker with people needlessly, even with beloved members of my family. I know You want so much more for me than that. In my quiet times, I can feel that divine urging to be more like You. Forgive me for the times I've stirred up trouble instead of goodwill. Please let Your supernatural peace seep into the depths of my soul, and then let the warmth and light of that peacemaking radiance stream like a ray of sunlight on a stormy day onto my family and to the world! Amen.

THINK ABOUT IT:
Is there someone in your life with whom the Holy Spirit might be encouraging you to make peace?

THE FINE ART OF NOISE

*Instruct the wise and they will be
wiser still; teach the righteous and
they will add to their learning.*

PROVERBS 9:9

Okay, so noise really isn't a fine art. . .is it, Lord?
But I'd like to do something artsy and useful
with noise, since my kids produce so much of it!
Actually, in all honesty, I want to hide in a deep,
dark—and quiet—closet. Maybe I even need a
vacation from motherhood. But since that may
not come right away, I turn to You, Lord, for
refreshment and calm. And for wisdom. Instruct
me so I may become a wiser mom. Show me how
to lovingly set boundaries with my kids and how
to balance our lives so that, rather than stress over
our days together, we might savor them! Amen.

THINK ABOUT IT:
What are some of the ways that God's wisdom
looks different from human wisdom?

I CAN FEEL THEM COMING

God is our refuge and strength,
an ever-present help in trouble.

PSALM 46:1

My dearest Lord, I can tell that the impending empty nest season of life is going to be one of the hardest battles of motherhood I will ever face! I was in the grocery store parking lot, and the moment I thought of my baby—a young woman now—driving away to start a new part of her life without me. . .well, I broke down sobbing right there. I can't go on like this, Lord. I need Your refuge and strength to endure this bittersweet passage in my life. I need Your understanding to deal with these complex emotions. Help me to see that her leaving to be independent, happy, and successful is a reflection of good mothering skills. Comfort me, Lord. Remind me that leaving does not mean she has stopped loving! Amen.

THINK ABOUT IT:
What conversations could you have with your grown child that might help you cope with the empty nest transition? What Bible verses might support you during this time?

THE POTHOLE OF PRIDE

*The L*ORD *Almighty has a day in store*
for all the proud and lofty, for all that is
exalted (and they will be humbled).

ISAIAH 2:12

I know we are born with cute little toes and cute
little noses; but in this fallen world, we are also
born with not-so-cute little egos. And, Lord, I know
that like everything else that grows, egos do too!
Help me to know how to humble myself before
You so You don't have to humble me. And help
me to train up my children to have confidence in
You without falling into a pothole of pride, to be
courageous without being arrogant, to be humble
without being weak. Such a pursuit in motherhood
seems impossible in this self-absorbed world. But
with You, all things are possible! Amen.

THINK ABOUT IT:
What can you do to show your kids that humility
is a beautiful trait? What Bible verses might help
you—and your kids—to become more humble?

THIS LIFE JOURNEY

*This is the account of Noah and his family.
Noah was a righteous man, blameless
among the people of his time, and he
walked faithfully with God.*

GENESIS 6:9

Lord, I acknowledge that this life journey is not merely in the physical realm. It is a spiritual walk too, and at times it is full of perilous twists and turns, fraught with dangers from my own willful choices, from living in a fallen world, and from the attacks of Satan. I confess that this spiritual trek is hard for me to understand and even harder for me to navigate. Please show me how to walk with You, just as Noah did—with faithfulness—and help me to show my children how to do so too. Amen.

THINK ABOUT IT:
In his walk with God, Noah showed his faithfulness by building an ark. What is one way you can show your faithfulness to God?

A BEAUTIFUL BUNDLE OF BLISS

The earth is full of his unfailing love.

PSALM 33:5

Heavenly Father, I love the way You love me. Unfailingly. Unconditionally. Lavishly. Eternally. Now that You've gifted me with a precious child, I sense Your love all over again. What a beautiful bundle of bliss. More wonderful than I could ever have imagined. Help me to always remember this moment. . .when she was first placed in my arms. When her tiny hand wrapped around my finger, her coos and gurgles made me chuckle, and her smile stole my heart. Let me always love my child as You have loved me. Even as the diapers pile up, the bills mount, and the nights become sleepless, never let me forget the miraculous wonder of this moment—this gift. Amen.

THINK ABOUT IT:
What are your favorite life moments with your children? Have you written some of them down? How have they reflected God's love for you?

A WONDERFUL GOD

Peter and the other apostles replied:
"We must obey God rather than human beings!"
ACTS 5:29

Lord, I confess that the word *obey* makes me squirm sometimes. To obey or submit to You, I'll have to *really* listen to You and Your Word. I may even have to give up my personal agenda. Why does that seem scary? Because I must secretly think that obeying You means I'll no longer be able to enjoy life. What a lie from the enemy—since You are the One who created joy in the first place! Without You, there is no wonder. No gifts. No miracles. None of the good things our spirits long for. Remind me daily, Lord, that the more I get to know You, the more the word *obey* will seem like the perfect and wonderful response to a perfect and wonderful God. Amen.

THINK ABOUT IT:
When you know you're in God's will, how do you feel, and what is the result?

THE ONGOING JUBILEE

*Whoever is patient has great understanding,
but one who is quick-tempered displays folly.*

PROVERBS 14:29

Lord, I always thought I was a patient woman.
Then I had kids. I'm in need of some serious help.
My kids are having fun, yes, but my house feels
out of control. Their friends come over—a lot—and
their idea of a good time is to unpack every last
toy, eat everything in the pantry, and make enough
rumbling noise to rattle all the dishes in my china
cabinet as well as my nerves! I'm afraid I'm about
to start screaming at everyone, and that isn't Your
way. Either I need to say no, learn how to stay calm
inside chaos, or find a balance between the two.
Help me, Lord, to be a patient mother to deal with
the ongoing jubilee. And give me wisdom to know
how to set sensible boundaries. Amen.

THINK ABOUT IT:
Do you think being patient is of one of the hardest
parts of being a mom? If so, how does honing in
on God's presence help?

HOW DO I LOVE YOU?

Love is patient, love is kind. It does not envy,
it does not boast, it is not proud. It does not
dishonor others, it is not self-seeking, it is not
easily angered, it keeps no record of wrongs.
Love does not delight in evil but rejoices with
the truth. It always protects, always trusts,
always hopes, always perseveres.

1 CORINTHIANS 13:4-7

Lord, it was easy to love my child when he cooed in my arms. When he blew bubbles in the bath or ran to me with posies. But now he's growing up, and he's almost a stranger. Once I even heard him mumble the words "I hate you." How do I love him now? I'm lost in pain, disillusionment, and anger. These teenage years are more than I can cope with. Show me how to take Your love passage in 1 Corinthians and make it part of our daily lives again. Lord, this mom needs a miracle. Amen.

THINK ABOUT IT:
Why does it often seem easier to hate than to love? How can you incorporate the power and nurture of God's love to overcome hate in your life?

RESENTMENT IS BUILDING

*Bear with each other and forgive one another
if any of you has a grievance against someone.
Forgive as the Lord forgave you.*

COLOSSIANS 3:13

My daughter totally forgot my birthday. *Sigh.* I am wounded, and I can feel the resentment building. I feel shuffled off, neglected. Lord, I know Your Word says I am to forgive others as You have forgiven me, and that is a good policy, but there is a strange comfort in my anger and in feeling sorry for myself. It's hard to give them up. But I want to do what is right and good in Your sight, Lord, so help me to move beyond my pettiness, to forgive her, and to find a time for some honest but loving dialogue about how moms love to be remembered on their special days. Amen.

THINK ABOUT IT:
Do you harbor any unforgiveness toward your child? How can you become as ready to forgive him or her as God has forgiven you?

A GIFT EXTRAORDINAIRE

Children are a heritage from the LORD,
offspring a reward from him.

PSALM 127:3

Through the years, I've been given big gifts and
little gifts, but none can come close to the one You
gave me, Lord—the day I discovered my child's
adorable smile, velvety head, and sweet baby love.
From that moment on, my heart turned into mush.
That is the essence of what I felt; and my prayer
is that You, Lord, will remind me of that feeling
when I have need—when the days and nights
don't feel quite as rosy as they once did. Let me
remember back to those early days after birth to
once again embrace this golden heritage—yes,
this baby gift extraordinaire! In Jesus' name I
pray. Amen.

THINK ABOUT IT:
What are some ways you can let your child know
what a God-gift he or she is?

GIVE ME COURAGE

*"Have I not commanded you? Be strong
and courageous. Do not be afraid;
do not be discouraged, for the Lord your
God will be with you wherever you go."*

JOSHUA 1:9

Lord, some days I feel more cowardly than courageous. In fact, I'm frightened by this world, because it seems to be coming apart at the seams. I'm scared of the darkness that seems to get more ominous by the week. And most of all, Lord, I'm scared for my kids. What kind of a world will they grow up in? Will it be a decent place? Or a place so fraught with sin's sickness that they will only be able to live an unfulfilled life—not the beautiful life You intended? Lord Jesus, still my racing heart. And give me courage. Remind me that wherever we go, You go with us as a family—and that is more than enough. Amen.

THINK ABOUT IT:
What does courage look like in today's world? During fearful times, how can you remind yourself of the power of God's presence with you?

HOW SHALL WE BEGIN?

Her children arise and call her blessed;
her husband also, and he praises her:
"Many women do noble things,
but you surpass them all."

PROVERBS 31:28–29

When I read about the Proverbs 31 woman, I admit, Lord, I am intimidated. To the max. I'm thinking, *Could that ever be me?* Could I do such noble deeds that my husband would rise up—even before his coffee—and shout my praises? And my kids too? I just can't imagine that. But the thing is, I really would like my life to be that way. I want to be a woman of noble deeds. Of substance and goodness. Yes, I want that. Please. What can I do to make that happen? Lord, how shall I begin? Amen.

THINK ABOUT IT:
What is one good and noble deed God might be nudging you to do today?

WHAT WILL HAPPEN?

"For I know the plans I have for you,"
declares the LORD, "plans to prosper
you and not to harm you,
plans to give you hope and a future."

JEREMIAH 29:11

Oh Lord, what does the future hold? I wonder—and I worry—about the future for my kids. I question what kind of a mom I'll be. What will my children grow up to be? Will they rebel and shun You, or will they embrace You as their Savior? What will happen to us as a family? Will we grow close or be driven apart by circumstances I can't even imagine yet? And so goes the fears of a mom in the middle of the night—and day. But in Your Word, You promise good things, a hope and a future. Help me to trust You fully so I can sleep soundly, knowing that the hours, days, and years ahead are in Your loving hands. Amen.

THINK ABOUT IT:
What fear can you give to God right now?

THAT KIND OF LOVE

For I am convinced that neither death nor life,
neither angels nor demons, neither the present
nor the future, nor any powers, neither height nor
depth, nor anything else in all creation, will be
able to separate us from the love of God
that is in Christ Jesus our Lord.

ROMANS 8:38-39

Lord, I appreciate Your love for me. The profound love You talk about in Romans 8 is just what I long for—all the way to my innermost being. It makes me want to rise up early and put a smile on the day. It helps me know I can call on You for whatever I need as a person—and as a mom. It reminds me that no matter what kind of horrors the world is embroiled in today, You are there, holding my hand, my heart, my life. I love You too! Amen.

THINK ABOUT IT:
What are some ways you can show your children how much God loves them?

WHEN WE THINK OF HONOR

"You know the commandments: 'You shall not commit adultery, you shall not murder, you shall not steal, you shall not give false testimony, honor your father and mother.'"

LUKE 18:20

Lord, I have read Your Ten Commandments, and I know You want children to honor their parents; but to be honest, some days I don't feel that "honored." That particular word seems to have lost its popularity in this modern age. When I think of being honored, it makes me think of respect, admiration, and devotion. But too many times my kids holler at me, ignore me, and disobey me. Lord, help me to encourage them to respect me and their father, but also, help me to give my children plenty of reasons to look up to, admire, and honor me. Amen.

THINK ABOUT IT:
What conversations have you had with your children about the Ten Commandments? Which of those commandments might God be wanting you to pray on?

A SERIOUS CASE OF THE GRINS

*A merry heart does good, like medicine,
but a broken spirit dries the bones.*

PROVERBS 17:22 NKJV

Oh, how I love it when the sun comes out bright and warm after a season of rain. It's so welcome, and it always does my heart good. For too long, Lord, I've been in a dreary mood—like those old dry bones the Bible talks about—and it's reflecting onto my family. Please help me learn how to have a merry heart and to teach my children how to enjoy a good belly laugh. The whole world needs a lot less scowls and a lot more smiles. And please let that serious case of the grins begin with me! Amen.

THINK ABOUT IT:
What activities can you do or what dialogue can you have with your children that will help you and them be merry at heart? How does it change your attitude knowing God would rather see a grin than a grimace?

PLUMB WORN OUT

Let us not become weary in doing good,
for at the proper time we will reap a
harvest if we do not give up.

GALATIANS 6:9

Okay, I've baked a casserole for my elderly neighbor. I've sewn costumes for my daughter's school play. I've volunteered at the local food pantry. I've worked my way into goodwill giddy gladness. Except, Lord, to be truly honest, I'm more harried than happy. I'm tired of doing so many nice things for so many people. In fact, no one appreciates all my hard work. I don't want to be a servant anymore. I don't see very many fringe benefits! Okay, I'm done with my pity party now. Lord, heal me of this negative attitude. Show me how to rest and be refreshed in You. Then bring me back to Your Word that tells me to not let myself get weary of doing good deeds for Your beloved. Amen.

THINK ABOUT IT:

What are some ways you can rest and refresh today so you can once again give with a joyful spirit? What Bible verse might reenergize you?

IN GOOD COMPANY

*He is despised and rejected by men, a Man
of sorrows and acquainted with grief. And we
hid, as it were, our faces from Him; He was
despised, and we did not esteem Him.*

ISAIAH 53:3 NKJV

Lord, I've heard You referred to in Your Word as
a "man of sorrows." I can't imagine the unthink-
able horrors You endured while You were here
on this earth. Sometimes when I watch the news,
as a witness of the world's ills, I feel a soulful sorrow too. The horrors of the world are all too
numerous to mention and too dark to fathom.
But I know that even in Your sorrow, You gave
the ultimate gift—Your perfect body for our sin-
stained ones. You offer us new life, real love, and
the bridge to heaven! Show me how to share
this glorious news with my children. And may
our lives become a daily celebration of Your
gift—Your glory. Amen.

THINK ABOUT IT:
Have you spent some time sharing with your
children about the birth, death, and resurrection
of Christ? How have you celebrated the gift of
Jesus today?

IT'S A ME-FIRST WORLD

*"In everything I did, I showed you that by
this kind of hard work we must help the weak,
remembering the words the Lord Jesus himself
said: 'It is more blessed to give than to receive.'"*

ACTS 20:35

Lord, I admit to sometimes succumbing to that selfish notion of wanting what I want when I want it. And having the mentality that I'd better "get while the getting is good." I know in my heart these life-slogans are not Your ways. Unfortunately, my kids have been watching me too closely, so they're starting to act and sound like me! That isn't always good. I think I need a mommy overhaul, and I give You permission right now to do it. And please, Lord, help me to remember Your teachings—that it is better to give than it is to receive. Amen.

THINK ABOUT IT:
In the past, how did it feel to share God's blessings with others? What are some ways you can teach your children about the joys of giving?

BRUISES THAT DON'T GO AWAY

But the wisdom that comes from heaven is first of all pure; then peace-loving, considerate, submissive, full of mercy and good fruit, impartial and sincere.

JAMES 3:17

Today I saw my little one tumble off his bike. He shed a few tears, and so did I. Maybe You did too, Lord. He'll probably get a bruise, but I'm glad it will heal quickly. That moment made me think of all the bruises he will get growing up—ones that I might not see. The verbal barbs that could affect him within. Perhaps the hurt will come from me—some harsh criticism that might wound his spirit—which he might carry with him always. Lord, please don't let it be so! Guard my tongue, and always let my words be pure and full of mercy and good fruit! Amen.

THINK ABOUT IT:

When anger rises and you feel some stinging words coming on, what are some things you can do instead of releasing a critical remark? What Bible verse might God want you to take to heart to help you in this endeavor?

THE GARDENER

*"I am the true vine, and my Father is the gardener.
He cuts off every branch in me that bears no fruit,
while every branch that does bear fruit he prunes
so that it will be even more fruitful."*

JOHN 15:1-2

I love being happy, Lord, but it's like a butterfly landing for a moment, and then it's gone. This is a fallen world, so I understand that perfect, unspoiled happiness will only be in heaven. But I do find myself wishing for more of it on earth too. I see in John 15 that You prune even the branches that bear fruit. *Ouch!* That sounds a bit painful. Please help me to realize that when I become holier from pruning, I will also find a more joyful way of life. Let me accept that truth—to embrace it—and to willingly change into whomever You created me to be as a woman, wife, and mother. Amen.

THINK ABOUT IT:
What are some ways that God has pruned you recently, and what were the results?

WHEN MOMS BEGIN TO JAW

Set a guard over my mouth, LORD;
keep watch over the door of my lips.

PSALM 141:3

I know the routine, Lord. Moms gather. They joke around. They laugh. They share their hearts in sweet fellowship. Good stuff. But sometimes, Lord, I know all too well what else can happen in those little circles of friendship—gossip. First, a few juicy words pop out, but with a bit of encouragement, what started out as a beneficial and amiable dialogue can turn into a rumormongering free-for-all! And I know, Lord, that gossip can have serious and permanent consequences. Hurt feelings. Destroyed relationships. Ruined reputations. On and on it goes. So please keep me from spewing gossip or even encouraging it. May I every day pray that You, Lord, "keep watch over the door of my lips"! Amen.

THINK ABOUT IT:
The last time you released a few morsels of gossip, what were the consequences? What did God teach you in that moment?

THE FACE OF COMPASSION

Therefore, as God's chosen people, holy and dearly loved, clothe yourselves with compassion, kindness, humility, gentleness and patience.

COLOSSIANS 3:12

Lord, what does compassion look like? Hmm. Do I remember to hold the door for an elderly person? Do I bake something yummy for the family that just moved into the neighborhood? Do I watch out for widows and orphans and feed the homeless? Do I really listen to friends? Really grieve with those who grieve? Am I teaching my kids how to be compassionate and kindhearted? I know it would be better for my kids to see these lovely attributes in me rather than preach sermons on the verse above. Lord, show me the way. I really would love to have my children see *Your* compassion adorning me! In Jesus' name I pray. Amen.

THINK ABOUT IT:
What was your last act of compassion that reflected Christ's?

I'M STILL FUMING

*Love is patient, love is kind. It does not envy,
it does not boast, it is not proud. It does not
dishonor others, it is not self-seeking, it is not
easily angered, it keeps no record of wrongs.*

1 Corinthians 13:4–5

Lord, the kids have splattered the wall with toothpaste, sassed me, dropped a gooey bowl of oatmeal, and deliberately flushed a toy down the toilet just to ponder the swirling dynamics of our new commode. They truly apologized for the hullabaloo, but I'm still fuming. I know in loving my kiddos, Lord, I shouldn't keep a record of wrongs. But those misdemeanors add up fast, and the list is sooo long! Then I remember that You let my list of wrongs fly away, never to be counted against me again. Okay, I get it, Lord. That record of transgressions against my kids? I'll go check out that new commode and officially flush that list! Amen.

THINK ABOUT IT:
When the Lord forgave you of your sins, how did that make you feel?

A PUDDLE IN THE CORNER

How long, LORD? Will you forget me forever?
How long will you hide your face from me?

PSALM 13:1

It's been one of those days, Lord. My friends seem to have abandoned me. My kids are rolling their eyes at me. My husband seems to be avoiding me. Is the whole world disgusted with me? Are You? I'm worried that You, too, will hide Your holy face from me. That You will forget me or run from me. I know if I were You, God, *I* would run from me! I'm discouraged. And disheartened. I've become no more than a puddle of tears in the corner. Help me, Lord. I don't even know exactly what to ask for. But in Your infinite knowledge and mercy, You know what I need. I will rest in that assurance always, just as David did all those many years ago. Amen.

THINK ABOUT IT:
What are some of the scriptures in Psalms that refer to David being rescued by God?

I CAN'T DO THIS
MOMMY THING ALONE

*I keep my eyes always on the L*ORD*. With him
at my right hand, I will not be shaken.*

PSALM 16:8

I didn't see it coming. I thought I knew best. I
got the idea that if I could memorize a handful
of scriptures, breathe a prayer from time to time,
and attend church services once a month—well,
that would take care of the spiritual part of my
mothering job. But that's when all the buttons
popped off of my mommy uniform, and I found
out the hard way that I can't do this mommy
thing alone. I need You, Lord, to help me every
day. Every hour. I have to keep my eyes on You,
Jesus, all the time. I need to hold Your hand not
only through the parenting years but all of my
life. Amen.

THINK ABOUT IT:

What are some ways you can teach your kids to
rely on the Lord all the time?

DOES MY SPIRIT GOOD

Endure hardship as discipline; God is treating you as his children. For what children are not disciplined by their father?

HEBREWS 12:7

Yes, Lord, I confess I did a bad thing. I disobeyed You, and I'm sorry. To be honest, some part of me doesn't want to face the consequences or take any correction from You. But just as I hope that my children will submit to my loving discipline, I come before You now, surrendering to You. I've learned over the years that even though Your reprimands might be painful for a short time, they do my spirit good in the end. For a good father disciplines his child. And I know that it would always be better to be chastised by You—the One who made me and loves me best—than to be praised mightily by the enemy of my soul. Amen.

THINK ABOUT IT:

Has God disciplined you recently? What did you learn from it?

A TREE OF LIFE

The soothing tongue is a tree of life,
but a perverse tongue crushes the spirit.
PROVERBS 15:4

Last week, Lord, my child came home from school with a scraped knee. I was sad to see it but glad that the wound healed quickly. Then I thought of all the tiny injuries we have on our hearts—those hidden from everyone but You, Lord. The ones that come from hurtful words. Proverbs says that a vicious tongue can crush a person's spirit; but on the other hand, soothing words are like a tree of life. What a difference! May my child always know I'm there for her when she has a hidden hurt, but more importantly may she know she can run to You with her every care—knowing Your healing touch will meet her there. Amen.

THINK ABOUT IT:
What injuries of the heart did you receive growing up? Have you let God heal them all?

LIVING FOREVER

But our citizenship is in heaven. And we eagerly await a Savior from there, the Lord Jesus Christ, who, by the power that enables him to bring everything under his control, will transform our lowly bodies so that they will be like his glorious body.

PHILIPPIANS 3:20-21

Lord, I know our society is always looking for the perfect supplement to live way beyond our years. Yes, long life is a gift, but if we truly had the choice, would we choose to live forever in this broken state? What would seem like a miracle would eventually become a curse, since we would long to shed these lowly bodies for glorious ones. Lord, may I show my kids how to live this life to the fullest with You by their side and how to be joyful, knowing as Christians that this fallen earth is not the last stop. Our citizenship is in heaven! Amen.

THINK ABOUT IT:
Have you told your child about the saving grace of Jesus Christ and the wonders of heaven?

RAIN DOWN ON ME

But the wisdom that comes from heaven is first of all pure; then peace-loving, considerate, submissive, full of mercy and good fruit, impartial and sincere.

JAMES 3:17

Lord, I confess, there are days when I am anything but wise. I can be a royal goof. And not just the guileless, funny kind of goof. I mean the kind You refer to in Proverbs as a fool—someone who has made decisions without knowledge, common sense, and biblical understanding. Lord, forgive me for my foolishness. Rain down on me with Your refreshing wisdom. I need a daily shower of it on my spirit. I know You love it when we ask for wisdom, so I humbly come before You now, seeking Your knowledge and understanding. Thank You, Lord! Amen.

THINK ABOUT IT:
How can you teach your children to be wise? What scriptures might you share with them?

CLOSE TO HIS HEART

He tends his flock like a shepherd:
he gathers the lambs in his arms
and carries them close to his heart;
he gently leads those that have young.

ISAIAH 40:11

Your words in Isaiah 40:11, Lord, are some of the most beautiful, tender, and heart-stirring in the Bible. What insight into Your love for me! What peace and joy I receive from this short passage! I can see that flock of bleating sheep, all of them plump and fluffy, bumping into each other as You ever so gently lead them safely along a stony path. I can see You, Lord, picking up one of the wanderers and bringing that little one up to Your heart, keeping her close, because that is what is needed. That is what is yearned for by the lamb and by the Shepherd. To be close. To be loved. To be always. Amen.

THINK ABOUT IT:
Think about a time when you felt that sweet, intimate closeness with the Great Shepherd.

A SOGGY OLD DISHTOWEL

*I can do all this through
him who gives me strength.*

PHILIPPIANS 4:13

As a mom, I am exhausted today, Lord. I have mounds of laundry to wash, meals to cook, diapers to change, cleaning, driving, shopping, and a dozen other chores. The problem is I don't even feel like getting out of bed! I'm not a mighty mom after all; instead I feel more like a soggy old dishtowel. Limp. Lifeless. And at risk of being tossed in the trash heap. So I come before You and ask for Your assistance—Your supernatural help. I need strength in every way, and I ask that You fulfill Your promise in Philippians 4:13. Ah, thank You, Lord. I accept Your strength. I rise up and thank You. Together, let us make this a joy-filled day to remember! Amen.

THINK ABOUT IT:
Name a time when you had to rely completely on the strength of the Lord.

GOD LOVES US INSIDE OUTSIDE

*For you created my inmost being; you knit
me together in my mother's womb.*

PSALM 139:13

Lord, I have been trying to explain to my child
about the upcoming birth of our second baby. It's
hard to explain to a wee one, but I used Your words
in Psalm 139:13, and there is some understanding
now as well as a bit of priceless insight. My child
sensed the love in that scripture—"You knit
me together in my mother's womb"—then she
pointed to my belly and said, "God loves us, inside
outside." It was one of those mothering moments
I will ponder in my heart always. It is a moment
worth recording and one for which I will thank
You, in all the days to come. Amen.

THINK ABOUT IT:
What are some wise things your children have
said that you could write down in a special baby
book? What things have you said that God may
have pondered in His heart?

FAR MORE THAN POSSESSIONS

Then he said to them, "Watch out! Be on your guard against all kinds of greed; life does not consist in an abundance of possessions."

LUKE 12:15

Lord, my kids are getting into a mode of wanting me to buy everything they see. Toys on TV, online, in stores at the mall, and in school—everywhere! I assumed this I-want-it-now stage was the world at work in my kids, and then I had some terrible thoughts: *Are they getting this materialistic mind-set from watching me? Do they see me buying lots and lots of unnecessary STUFF? Belongings that end up in a garage sale months later?* Search every part of me, Lord, for greedy little inclinations and help me to rid myself of them. Remind me that life is far more than mere possessions! Amen.

THINK ABOUT IT:
Rather than store-bought toys, what are some homemade games and playthings that you and your kids can make together? What things might God be prompting you to share with others?

EMOTIONAL BAGGAGE

Jesus replied, "No one who puts a hand to the plow and looks back is fit for service in the kingdom of God."

LUKE 9:62

Lord, I want my kids to grow up in a joyful, creative, and active home, but they can't do that if I'm dragging emotional baggage around with me. It's wearing me out spiritually—and, as it turns out, physically. I'm exhausted. I'm at Your mercy, which I know is the very best place to be. You remind us in Your Word that if we are constantly looking back, we won't be fit for service in Your kingdom. So please remove any emotional baggage in me that is keeping me bound to the past and unable to move forward. I accept Your healing touch. I praise You for Your supernatural freedom. I embrace it fully! Amen.

THINK ABOUT IT:
How is God helping you move forward? How can you help your kids from being bogged down with emotional baggage in the future?

MY HIDING PLACE

*You are my hiding place; you will protect
me from trouble and surround me
with songs of deliverance.*

PSALM 32:7

Lord, I sense danger all around my family, and
I'm scared. I hear about terrible accidents of all
kinds. I see children growing up in rebellion. I
even hear about young people taking their own
lives. These terrors are just a glimpse of what
can go wrong with a family—and it sometimes
paralyzes me with fear. I know we are not to live
with anxiety and dread, Lord, so I will choose to
put my trust in You. Please protect our family
from harm and evil. Surround us with Your loving
care and Your songs of deliverance. And when
You do allow trouble to pass through our lives,
stay near us, help us to bear it, and please work
it for Your, and ultimately our, good. Amen.

THINK ABOUT IT:
How did the Lord help you when you or a family
member were going through a rough time?

YOUR PEACE

*"All your children will be taught by
the L*ORD*, and great will be their peace."*

ISAIAH 54:13

Oh Lord, many days it feels as if our world is spinning out of control. I've tried to shelter my children from the division and hatred around us, but the task is getting harder by the day. They see discord everywhere and are beginning to talk about it. I'm concerned that this abrasive and conflict-ridden society of ours will influence my family. I think it already has. I want my children to be taught by You, Lord, so please allow Your Holy Spirit to give me the right words to say; help me to use those teachable moments wisely and to live a life that exemplifies Your biblical precepts. I pray that peace—Your peace that passes all understanding—will rain down on our family. Amen.

THINK ABOUT IT:

How is the peace of God different from the peace the world promotes?

FINDING BALANCE

*Fathers, do not embitter your children,
or they will become discouraged.*

COLOSSIANS 3:21

Lord, I find every aspect of parenting to be difficult at times, but understanding the right way to discipline my children has to be one of the hardest parts to wrestle with. If I'm too lenient with my kids, they might become idle and disrespectful and run me over like a bulldozer! But if I'm constantly nagging at them to improve their behavior they might become discouraged and embittered, and then give up. What am I to do? Help me find the right balance in my corrections, and help my kids find comfort in godly parameters. As You have so graciously shown me unconditional love in all You do for me, remind me to show my children unconditional love in all I do for them. Amen.

THINK ABOUT IT:
When was the last time God disciplined you? How did it make you feel?

HELP US AS A FAMILY

He declared to you his covenant, the Ten Commandments, which he commanded you to follow and then wrote them on two stone tablets.

DEUTERONOMY 4:13

Lord, I continue to see news reports of Your Ten Commandments being removed from public places. I also see that many people do not even know what Your commandments are, let alone follow them. Honestly, I've become afraid for our country. I'm also afraid for my children as they grow up in a secular nation rather than the one founded on biblical principles. Without You, Lord, we are doomed. Help me to do my part in teaching Your commandments to my children and relating them to others when possible. Help us as a family to love You and Your laws and to be willing to stand up to proclaim them, no matter the cost. Amen.

THINK ABOUT IT:
Have you memorized the Ten Commandments? Have you taught them to your children?

A SUPER-HONEST MOMENT

*May these words of my mouth and this
meditation of my heart be pleasing in your
sight, LORD, my Rock and my Redeemer.*

PSALM 19:14

If we're going to have a super-honest moment,
Lord, here it is: I wouldn't want my friends and
neighbors to hear me behind closed doors. I can
really let it rip with some ugly verbiage. On top
of that, my thought life is a mess at times—full of
vain imaginings, less than lovely ponderings, and
serious doubts about You (just to name a few).
But I also know there is no such thing as "behind
closed doors" with You. All is laid bare for You to
hear and see. Oh Lord, I come to You, knowing
these truths, and I ask You to make Psalm 19:14
my life verse. Please write these words on my
heart and help me follow them diligently. Amen.

THINK ABOUT IT:
In what ways might you tend to become two very
different people: one who puts on a pious face
in public and a different one at home? How can
knowing that God sees all help you be wholly
pleasing to Him?

EVERY GOOD AND PERFECT GIFT

Every good and perfect gift is from above, coming down from the Father of the heavenly lights, who does not change like shifting shadows.

JAMES 1:17

Dear Lord, today I have cleaned and cooked and driven and listened and taught and disciplined and tended and mended. . .and then dropped in exhaustion. Sometimes I get so bogged down in the mundane chores of motherhood that I forget how blessed this calling really is. I acknowledge that every good gift comes from You, Father, and that being a mom is a truly great one! Even after a very long day, help me to always remember that truth—that mothering is a noble calling, full of wonder and mystery and laughter and beauty! In Jesus' name I pray. Amen.

THINK ABOUT IT:
Have you told your kids lately what an amazing gift from God they are? Do so today!

THE BEAUTIFUL FEET

*And how can anyone preach unless they
are sent? As it is written: "How beautiful
are the feet of those who bring good news!"*

ROMANS 10:15

Lord, I want my children to know You as their Lord
and Savior, so please guide my words as I share
the Gospel. Soften their hearts with Your Holy
Spirit so they will be receptive to Your message
of salvation. Then teach our family how to witness
to others. It's easy for me to share recipes and
tell women about the finest pediatricians, the
heathiest snacks, the most educational toys, and
the best baby guidebooks, but it's not so easy
to share the Gospel. Beginning with me, please
show our family how to be the "beautiful feet"
that take the good news to a hurting world! Amen.

THINK ABOUT IT:
Have your children accepted Christ as their
Savior? Do you take the time to tell others of His
wondrous love and grace?

YOU ARE *THE* WAY

Jesus answered, "I am the way and the truth and the life. No one comes to the Father except through me."

JOHN 14:6

Lord, throughout history, some people have tried to run from Your message of salvation, or they try to poison it by saying that in the end, everyone will go to heaven, regardless of what religion they choose. But I have read Your Word—the Bible—and I know You make it very clear that You, Jesus, are the truth. You are the life. And You are the *only* way to heaven. As a mom and concerned Christian, help me to know how to keep my children safe from the world's dangerous dilution of Your message and how I can pray for a sinful world that needs Your beautiful truth, Your merciful forgiveness, and Your everlasting life! Amen.

THINK ABOUT IT:
When you gather around the table for family meals, how can you promote a discussion of current issues, scriptures, and truth?

I HAVE CALLED YOU FRIENDS!

"I no longer call you servants, because a servant does not know his master's business. Instead, I have called you friends, for everything that I learned from my Father I have made known to you."

JOHN 15:15

My kids have a lot of friends, Lord, and even though I love them all, I admit some of them aren't a good influence. Please give me wisdom concerning this matter, and help me to share the truth with my children that You, Lord, are the best friend they will ever know. Impress upon their hearts even through adulthood, that wherever they are or whatever they have done, You are there for them and will love them even better than me who loves them greatly. Thank You, Lord, for loving and standing by my kids. Amen.

THINK ABOUT IT:
What kind of friends do *you* have? Are they a good influence on your family? Are you a God-influence on them?

THE EVERLASTING GOD!

Do you not know? Have you not heard? The LORD
is the everlasting God, the Creator of the ends
of the earth. He will not grow tired or weary,
and his understanding no one can fathom.

ISAIAH 40:28

Oh Lord, my God, when I look at Your handiwork, I am spellbound. Mesmerized by the luminosities of Your night sky. Fascinated by Your world under a microscope. Captivated by Your dragonflies, ghost fish, and wombats. Your majestic mountain spires, shimmering seas, and underwater caves. I cannot fathom the vastness and details of Your creation, Your knowledge, Your power. And I cannot comprehend Your love for us. . .for me. I am such a tiny dot in Your vast universe, and yet I can feel Your tender love for me and my family. I love You, God, and I offer You my profoundly grateful heart. In Jesus' name I pray. Amen.

THINK ABOUT IT:
What part of God's creation do you love the most and why?

SHINE YOUR LIGHT

Woe to those who call evil good and good evil,
who put darkness for light and light for darkness,
who put bitter for sweet and sweet for bitter.

ISAIAH 5:20

I watch the news, Lord, and I shiver in my soul.
I watch my fellow man bickering, fist-fighting,
plotting evil schemes, and I shake my head.
Sometimes I look in the mirror, Lord, and I don't
even know myself; I see, within the shadows of
my spirit, sin that needs to be forgiven. Many
people have come to a place where they call evil
"good" and good "evil." It's a poisonous switch
in morality that will destroy our souls if we let it.
Please deliver us from evil and shine Your light
in all the dark crevices of our hearts. We need You
now, Lord Jesus! Come! Amen.

THINK ABOUT IT:
What are some moral choices society calls good
that are really evil in the eyes of the Lord? How
might you shine some of God's light onto them?

A CURE FOR THE GIMMIES

*And do not forget to do good and to share with
others, for with such sacrifices God is pleased.*
HEBREWS 13:16

Lord, sometimes my children are pretty demanding about what they want. They have even
stomped their little feet and hollered at me when
I said no. It's so embarrassing when they do that
in public. Then I remember that when I don't get
the answers to my prayers just when I want them,
I act a bit like that. Maybe not with a tantrum, but
in my heart things get a little dicey. I'm sorry for
that, Lord, when I succumb to this prevailing self-
indulgent, give-it-to-me-now mentality. Maybe a
cure for the "gimmies" is to take Hebrews 13:16 to
heart, which would help to switch my perspective
from me, myself, and I to *others*. Please teach my
children—please teach *me*—to do good and share
with those in need. Amen.

THINK ABOUT IT:
What could you do as a family to help someone
in need? How can you keep Hebrews 13:16 fresh
in your family's mind?

TALKING TO GOD

Pray continually.
1 THESSALONIANS 5:17

Lord, when You say we should "pray continually," what does that mean exactly? Maybe You mean that when I see an ambulance on the way to work I should pray for those who've been hurt. Or when I experience tension at church or my child is struggling with homework, I need to ask You to work in our midst. Or when sin comes calling, I should ask for Your help in resisting those temptations throughout the day. Or as I witness a sunset that ignites the evening sky with color, perhaps I should breathe a prayer of thanksgiving. Maybe praying frequently isn't giving up my time, but fellowshipping with the One who has the power to work all things for my good, the One who loves me best, the One who can forgive my sins, and the One who is worthy of my praise. Lord, may I never stop fellowshipping with You! Amen.

THINK ABOUT IT:
What are some ways you "pray continually" throughout the day?

SWEET FREEDOM

"Therefore, if you are offering your gift at the altar and there remember that your brother or sister has something against you, leave your gift there in front of the altar. First go and be reconciled to them; then come and offer your gift."

MATTHEW 5:23–24

Lord, why is saying "I'm sorry" so hard? Even the thought of making amends with a coworker, my husband, children, friends, or church members makes me sweat. I guess it's pride. Nobody likes to admit to being the bad guy. It's so much more satisfying to know *I've* been wronged. But the bottom line is that I want to follow Your teachings, Lord; and I can see in Matthew 5 that You'd like people to make amends, whether it is an apology, a reparation, or whatever might make the relationship right again. Please help me learn that I am not ensnared by reconciliation but am, on the contrary, given sweet freedom in it. Amen.

THINK ABOUT IT:
Is there someone with whom you need to make amends? How does it help knowing that you must forgive others to receive God's forgiveness?

MUSIC FROM YOUR HEART!

*Speaking to one another with psalms, hymns,
and songs from the Spirit. Sing and make
music from your heart to the Lord.*

EPHESIANS 5:19

Lord, if I suddenly burst out into song, my kids would think I'd lost my mind. *And* I have a tin ear, which makes my voice sound more like a wail than a croon. But maybe You just want a joyful noise and a willing heart. Well, *that* I can do. I want to rejoice in the new day, Lord, and I want to praise You for everything You do, since You are worthy of my worship. I suppose if my family can shout cheers at sporting events with utter abandon, then we can learn to sing praises to You, the Almighty! Amen.

THINK ABOUT IT:

What are some ways you can make music to the Lord?

WHEN I'M TEMPTED

Finally, brothers and sisters, whatever is true, whatever is noble, whatever is right, whatever is pure, whatever is lovely, whatever is admirable—if anything is excellent or praiseworthy—think about such things.

PHILIPPIANS 4:8

Lord, the next time I scratch my head concerning how to pick and choose over the world's various forms of entertainment, please remind me of the above verse so that I can help guide our family with good sense. I am painfully aware that much of what society considers family-friendly fun is far from it. Artists tend to think that if they created it—whatever medium it is—then it's worthy of an audience. I know from experience that this ideology isn't true. Lord, when I'm tempted to be careless about entertainment for me and my family, prompt me to search for whatever is true, right, pure, lovely, and admirable above all other things. Amen.

THINK ABOUT IT:
In the past, what form of entertainment has had a negative or positive impact on your family? How can you keep your mind set on God's goodness?

HOW TO GROW A CHILD

All Scripture is God-breathed and is useful for teaching, rebuking, correcting and training in righteousness, so that the servant of God may be thoroughly equipped for every good work.

2 TIMOTHY 3:16–17

Lord, I've noticed that mothers seem to spout a lot of advice and can get downright pushy about it. Then there are the mountains of self-help books that promise to teach me how to grow a child in ten easy steps, yet the authors of such tomes don't always agree. On top of that, experts on parenting often assure me I'm doing a myriad of things wrong. So I am going to skip the manuals and go straight to Your good book to discover how *You* grow a child in wisdom and stature. Your parenting advice is stellar, time-tested, and, even better, it's given in love and not judgment. Thank You, Lord, for not only giving me my children, but showing me the way they—and I—should go. Amen.

THINK ABOUT IT:
What are some of your favorite scriptures on how to grow a child up in the Lord?

THE SUBLIME BEAUTY OF GOD

*One thing I ask from the L*ORD*, this only do I seek: that I may dwell in the house of the L*ORD *all the days of my life, to gaze on the beauty of the L*ORD *and to seek him in his temple.*

PSALM 27:4

Psalm 27 tells me You are beautiful, Lord. You are sublime—exalted and transcendent and glorious! And Your creation is exquisite as well. Because I am made in Your image, I want to be more like You in every way. I want to create a life of beauty all around me, whether it emanates from my hands as art, or from my heart as an offering. Oh Lord, my God, I want to know the essence of who You are on a deeper level so that I can live a life of beauty! Amen.

THINK ABOUT IT:
What can you create with your children today (whether from your hands or your heart) that will celebrate the beauty of God and His creation?

EMPOWERED BY YOU

*But God made the earth by his power; he
founded the world by his wisdom and stretched
out the heavens by his understanding.*

JEREMIAH 10:12

Lord, society keeps telling me I'm supposed to be
empowered. But by whom? *Me?* I'm certainly not
powerful enough for such a monstrous mission.
Or I'm told I should take control of my life. Yet
what human really governs anything in this life? If
humans appear to be in full command, it's only an
illusion. I know that You, God, are truly in control
of all things. You made the whole universe with
Your supernatural power—and You made me. I
surrender to that truth. I acknowledge You as the
Maker of all things, and I choose to be empowered
by You alone, God! Guide my every step. Amen.

THINK ABOUT IT:
Have you given God full control of all areas of
your life?

TO LEAD A QUIET LIFE

And to make it your ambition to lead a quiet life:
You should mind your own business and work
with your hands, just as we told you.

1 THESSALONIANS 4:11

Lord, I know some women who live large and loud, needing to be the center of attention all the time. And they are not content to merely bask in the limelight, but they love to get in my face and tell me about my every flaw—in colorful detail. These women lead anything but quiet lives. They could even be accused of noise pollution! But just in case that woman—on a rare occasion—happens to be me, please control my tongue and remind me to make it my aim to lead a quiet life, mind my own business, and get down to work! In Jesus' name I pray. Amen.

THINK ABOUT IT:
How could this advice from Thessalonians be a more freeing and productive way to live? Why not incorporate it into your life today?

THE PERFECT FOOTHOLD

"In this manner, therefore, pray: Our Father in heaven, hallowed be Your name. Your kingdom come. Your will be done on earth as it is in heaven. Give us this day our daily bread. And forgive us our debts, as we forgive our debtors. And do not lead us into temptation, but deliver us from the evil one. For Yours is the kingdom and the power and the glory forever. Amen."

MATTHEW 6:9–13 NKJV

Lord, I want my children to know how to pray. They already know they can come to You anytime, anywhere, and talk to You as a beloved Father. But I know the prayer Jesus taught us to pray is the perfect foothold as we journey along in our requests to You. Help me to memorize this holy prayer in Your Word and to teach it to my children. Then let it always be in our hearts as a family.

THINK ABOUT IT:
Do your kids enjoy talking to God? If not, how can you make it more enjoyable for them?

THE WONDERFUL DAYS TO COME

*"Here I am! I stand at the door and knock.
If anyone hears my voice and opens the
door, I will come in and eat with that
person, and they with me."*

REVELATION 3:20

I imagine it like this, Lord: I iron my finest tablecloth, and I put out my best china. I cook my most beloved dish, and I pull out the chair at the head of the table—for You. I don't need to worry that You'll be late. You come to eat with me, and we talk about our relationship to each other and our Father God. And we toast to all the love and joy and all the wonderful days to come. Thank You, Lord, for coming to be with me, to sup with me, to live a life hand in hand with me. So beautiful is that life, in fact, that I'm looking forward to an eternity of it! Amen.

THINK ABOUT IT:
How can you show your children that Christianity is not a religion but a relationship?

MY BUMBLY WAYS

We all, like sheep, have gone astray, each of us has turned to our own way; and the LORD has laid on him the iniquity of us all.

ISAIAH 53:6

Sometimes when I look at the reckless and random ways people live their lives, it looks sort of muddled from the outside. Maybe it looks muddled from the inside too. Is that the way I live my life, Lord? Am I guilty of going my own way willy-nilly? Have I become that little sheep full of bumbly ways—too silly and senseless to even know the perils all around me? If so, I am sorry, Lord. Please forgive me. And help me see the benefits of staying near to You and Your loving guidance as the Good Shepherd of my soul. Amen.

THINK ABOUT IT:
How do you know when you've gone astray from the Good Shepherd? And what do you do about it?

TONIGHT I AM THAT WAVE

But when you ask, you must believe and not doubt, because the one who doubts is like a wave of the sea, blown and tossed by the wind.

JAMES 1:6

Oh dear Lord, tonight I confess that I am that wave You talk about in James 1:6. Forgive me. My doubts are causing me to get hammered and hurled by the wind. When this occurs, why is it usually in the night? Is it because there is no light or warmth from the sun? Is it because Satan works harder to discourage us because he knows we feel more vulnerable in the darkness? Or do we think that slumber seems like a form of death, and secretly, it frightens us? Whatever the reason, Lord, I ask You to calm those waves of doubts and fear right now with Your supernatural power. In Jesus' name I pray. Amen.

THINK ABOUT IT:
When do doubts plague you, and how do you handle them? What scripture might you memorize to help you fend off uncertainties?

WHEN I SAY GOODBYE

Her children arise and call her blessed;
her husband also, and he praises her:
"Many women do noble things,
but you surpass them all."

PROVERBS 31:28-29

Lord, when I say a final goodbye to this old world—
and I know that day will come for all of us—I
wonder what people will say about me. When they
gather to say a handful of words that summarize
my years here, what will those words be? How
will friends and relatives remember me? For my
wisdom and acts of kindness and faith? Or will
their memory recall a woman of less virtue? Lord,
help me in this. I really do want to live a life that
reflects Your love. Help me to live in such a noble
way, to be such a reflection of You that people will
know me to be a blessing wherever I go. Amen.

THINK ABOUT IT:
How do you want to be remembered? How can you
become more of a blessing—to God and others?

YOUR PROMISES

"Be strong and courageous. Do not be
afraid or terrified because of them,
for the LORD your God goes with you;
he will never leave you nor forsake you."

DEUTERONOMY 31:6

I have found this world to be a dangerous place, Lord. I'm concerned that after my kids grow up to love You as their Lord and then go out into the world, they will get battered spiritually in every possible way. What if they join a cult? What if they are tempted by one of the many false prophets who claim to be You? In other words, I need to world-proof my kids! I come to You with my concerns, Lord. I choose to trust You when You say You will go with us wherever we go. That You will never forsake us. I will trust in Your promises for my children and for me. Amen.

THINK ABOUT IT:
What are some ways you can pray for your children today?

FEELING USED UP

Jesus replied: " 'Love the Lord your God with all your heart and with all your soul and with all your mind.' This is the first and greatest commandment."

MATTHEW 22:37–38

I admit, God, that there are days I don't feel loved by my kids. They come to me for requests—a mother lode of them. They come to me for help, cash, new toys, cash, clean socks, cash. I feel used up at times. I recently had this niggling thought: *Is this what my prayer time looks like?* You know, when I ask for more and more stuff to make my life smoother, healthier, better—and maybe a little richer? Sometimes I forget to be Your child. To just love You as *I* always dream of being loved by my kids. Forgive me, Lord. Remind me to run into Your loving arms. To be still at times and know You are God. To love and be loved by You. Amen.

THINK ABOUT IT:
What ways can you show God how much you love Him?

TIME IN ETERNITY

You make known to me the path of life;
you will fill me with joy in your presence,
with eternal pleasures at your right hand.

PSALM 16:11

From a young age, Lord, we realize that somewhere a clock is ticking, ever counting time, reminding us of closure. Although I find joy in a blossoming fragrant rose, I watch it fade all too quickly. And as I relish an achingly beautiful passage of music, I know with lingering sadness that it, too, must end. All the memorable, beautiful moments come to a close. But I thank You, Lord, that there is life beyond this transitory earth! I choose You, Jesus, as my Lord of all; and in doing so, I choose eternity with You, where beauty, delight, and wonder will never fade or end. So I'm going to stop obsessing over that clock now, because You and I have forever together. Amen.

THINK ABOUT IT:
Have you chosen Christ as your Savior? Do you celebrate your eternal heritage?

THE EPIC BATTLE

*For our struggle is not against flesh and
blood, but against the rulers, against the
authorities, against the powers of this dark
world and against the spiritual forces
of evil in the heavenly realms.*

EPHESIANS 6:12

All is quiet in the house, Lord, as I come before
You. My heart content, I take joy in Your presence
and feel Your everlasting peace. But I sense an epic
battle raging around us in the spiritual realm. So
I pray for me and my family members, Lord, that
You would place Your divine protection around
each of us: physically, mentally, and spiritually.
Please watch over us so that we might go out into
the world—to fulfill our calling, to delight in Your
wondrous creation, and to proclaim Your good
news—but without giving in to the temptations of
this world or surrendering to the enemy! Amen.

THINK ABOUT IT:
What are some earthly manifestations of this
spiritual battle, and in what ways has it influenced
your family? What scriptures can you memorize
to keep you and your thoughts in God's light?

THE EMPTY-NEST BLUES

"A time is coming and in fact has come when you will be scattered, each to your own home. You will leave me all alone. Yet I am not alone, for my Father is with me."

JOHN 16:32

Lord, I confess my soul is singing the empty-nest blues. That mothering nature is so deeply embedded in me that I'm having trouble letting go. Good thing I have You on my side, Lord. I can't do this empty-nest thing without You. Thank You that when my children move on with their own lives and families, I am not alone. You go with me all the days of my life. Be near me, Jesus, and show me how to sing a new song. Help this life transition to be filled with new opportunities, adventures, and ways to serve You! Amen.

THINK ABOUT IT:
What are some things you have always wanted to do but never had the time? How does it feel knowing that through thick or thin, God will never leave you?

YOU DELIGHT IN ME?

"The LORD your God is with you, the Mighty
Warrior who saves. He will take great delight
in you; in his love he will no longer rebuke you,
but will rejoice over you with singing."

ZEPHANIAH 3:17

That's a mind-boggling thought, Lord—that You
take delight in me. I know I take merry pleasure
in my kids. In their funny peekaboo antics under
their makeshift tent made of blankets. Their crayon
masterpieces, which are currently on exhibit, taped
to the refrigerator door. Their giddy, skipping
runs as they make a kite lift off the ground and fly
into the wild blue yonder. I love it. Is that the way
You see me, Lord? With genuine delight? Hard to
imagine, and yet my spirit longs to understand
this truth and celebrate it. Praise You, Lord, for
Your love. It inspires me, woos me, comforts and
sustains me. Amen.

THINK ABOUT IT:
What are some of the ways you bring God delight?
What are some ways your children bring *you*
delight?

EVEN AT A YOUNG AGE

*Each of you should use whatever gift you have
received to serve others, as faithful stewards
of God's grace in its various forms.*

1 PETER 4:10

Lord, You've given each of my children special talents. They amaze me at every turn! Even at a young age I could see Your hand on them as I watched them grow into their unique gifts. Thank You, Lord, for Your faithfulness to our family. Please help my kids take these dreams as far as You want them to go. Give them perseverance and purpose, and help them to be faithful stewards, remembering to always use their many gifts to help serve others for Your glory. In Jesus' name I pray. Amen.

THINK ABOUT IT:

What gifts do you use to serve God? What surprised you as your children began to show their various interests and abilities?

YOU ARE MINDFUL OF ME!

When I consider your heavens, the work of your fingers, the moon and the stars, which you have set in place, what is mankind that you are mindful of them, human beings that you care for them?

PSALM 8:3-4

Thank You, Lord, that You are mindful of me and my family. That You care for us deeply. When I think of the vastness of Your heavens, I am filled with profound awe, and I wonder how it is that You can love us all so dearly—as if we are each a priceless treasure. Thank You for humbling Yourself to be born into our world, to live among us, and then to sacrifice everything for our good. Thank You for Your precious gift. . .Your unfathomable love. Amen.

THINK ABOUT IT:
What are the various ways you experience God's love for you? How does His love change your life?

I AM TRULY SORRY

"This is what the LORD says: 'When people fall down, do they not get up? When someone turns away, do they not return?'"

JEREMIAH 8:4

Lord, I confess that sometimes I fall down on the job of being a good mom. I might lose my patience and my temper from time to time, and I might raise my voice a teeny bit. (Or maybe a lot.) I might do a variety of things that are—well, un-momlike and not very Christlike. I am truly sorry, Lord. I humbly repent, and I ask for Your forgiveness. Please let me have a do-over. Let me become the mom You dreamed of me being the day my child was born! Amen.

THINK ABOUT IT:
Is there anything you need to ask God to forgive you for? Do you owe your children an apology?

WITH ALL YOUR HEART

Whatever you do, work at it with all your heart, as working for the Lord, not for human masters.

COLOSSIANS 3:23

One of the many things our society needs is balance, Lord—even in the area of work. Some people choose to work so little they aren't able to feed their families, while others make their careers such a top priority that they hardly get to *see* their families! Neither one of those ways is going to work properly. Please help me to be an example of Your biblical teachings. Show me how to encourage my children to live by working with all their heart for *You*, not their overseers, that they might know the pleasure that comes from pleasing You! In Jesus' name I pray. Amen.

THINK ABOUT IT:
What is a chore that you can do together with your children that could create a teachable moment concerning this topic of how you, as God's children, should view work?

THE WORDS OF MY MOUTH

My son, keep your father's command and do not forsake your mother's teaching. Bind them always on your heart; fasten them around your neck.

PROVERBS 6:20-21

Dearest Lord, if my children are to listen to my words very carefully and bind them to their hearts, then please let my advice and teaching be infused with biblical wisdom. I'm going to need Your insight and understanding in every area of my life—and theirs. It's easy to see that being a mom is a wonderful, but slightly terrifying, endeavor! Some days it feels as though I am a breath away from saying the wrong thing, so please help me to think and pray before I offer counsel! In Jesus' name I pray. Amen.

THINK ABOUT IT:
Do your children listen to what you say, take your advice to heart, and benefit from it? Do you listen to and take to heart what God speaks into your life?

INDEED, JUST PASSING THROUGH

*For our light and momentary troubles
are achieving for us an eternal glory
that far outweighs them all.*

2 CORINTHIANS 4:17

I am so weary, Lord. My burden seems too heavy, the pain too intense, and the grief and loss too much to bear. Be very near me, Jesus, in all I am going through. Tenderly remind me that we are merely sojourners in this life. We are indeed just passing through. As a Christian I have the assurance that after these dusty travels are finally done, my home is in heaven. "Home, sweet home" will have a new, profound meaning, beauty beyond belief, and there will be an eternity of joy unspeakable! Thank You for that promise, Lord, and the peace it brings. In Jesus' name I pray. Amen.

THINK ABOUT IT:
What are you looking forward to most about heaven?

THOSE SCARY MOM MOMENTS

"The Lord himself goes before you and will be with you; he will never leave you nor forsake you. Do not be afraid; do not be discouraged."

DEUTERONOMY 31:8

It's not possible, Lord, for me to be with my kids every second of every day, and even when I'm watching over them, I know all too well that bad things can still happen, whether physically, mentally, or spiritually. That's why my children must learn that even though I love them deeply, You are the One, Lord, they must grow to trust with every aspect of their Christian lives. Let them know that wherever they go, You will never leave them nor forsake them. In Jesus' name I pray. Amen.

THINK ABOUT IT:
What concerns you the most about raising children? Does this verse in Deuteronomy 31:8 help you deal with the many uncertainties of mothering?

YOUR GENTLE MERCIES

Lord my God, I called to you
for help, and you healed me.

PSALM 30:2

My child is ill, Lord, and it's so painful to see. If it were possible, I would take on my child's illness rather than see him suffer. Then I realize that You love my child even more than I do. So I call out to You for divine help and healing. I believe You can make my child well! Please draw near to us, Lord Jesus, I pray. Surround my child with Your loving presence and Your powerful, healing touch. Please bring him a good night's sleep, and may our morning be bright with joy. I thank You for hearing my petition and for Your gentle mercies. Praise be to Your holy name! Amen.

THINK ABOUT IT:
When was the last time you asked God for healing? How did He answer your prayer?

THE STONES WILL CRY OUT!

"Blessed is the king who comes in the name of the Lord!" "Peace in heaven and glory in the highest!" Some of the Pharisees in the crowd said to Jesus, "Teacher, rebuke your disciples!" "I tell you," he replied, "if they keep quiet, the stones will cry out."

LUKE 19:38-40

When I think of Your creation, Lord, and Your miracles, Your unfailing love, and Your death on the cross for my redemption, I want to raise my hands in praise. All of creation exalts You, and so should I! When I get the spiritual nudge to do so, let me raise my voice to praise You, Lord. May I sing a new song and even dance before You as David did. For You are the King of kings and Lord of lords. May all glory and honor and praise be Yours. Hallelujah! Amen.

THINK ABOUT IT:

What are some ways you can praise God for all He has done for you and your family?

SUCH LOVE!

You have searched me, Lord, and you know me. You know when I sit and when I rise; you perceive my thoughts from afar. You discern my going out and my lying down; you are familiar with all my ways. Before a word is on my tongue you, Lord, know it completely. You hem me in behind and before, and you lay your hand upon me. Such knowledge is too wonderful for me, too lofty for me to attain.

Psalm 139:1–6

Oh Lord, when I read Your love note to me in Psalm 139, I can't contain my delight—that You could love me so dearly. You not only created me but continue to know every detail surrounding my life. And You still love me and want to be with me! Yes, such knowledge is too wonderful for me to understand, but oh, how I love to hear it. Thank You, Lord. Amen.

THINK ABOUT IT:
What are some ways God has shown His love for you and your family?

I WILL LISTEN

*"Then you will call on me and come and
pray to me, and I will listen to you."*

JEREMIAH 29:12

Oh Lord, I am weary from the clamor and chatter
of this world. Everyone seems to be shouting
these days, desperate to be heard. They want us to
listen, to understand, to empathize. . .all day, every
day. I am about to collapse from all the appeals
and demands, but then I see Your divine words:
"I will listen." Those have to be three of the most
beautiful words ever put together. Imagine, You,
the Creator of the universe, willing to listen to
me, whether I'm having a fine day or a foul one.
Thank You, Lord, for this most precious blessing
called "listening." Amen.

THINK ABOUT IT:
Why do you think God wants to listen to His
children? What are some of the things you need
to talk to Him about today?

AUNT GERTRUDE

*"But I tell you, love your enemies and
pray for those who persecute you."*

MATTHEW 5:44

Life can be sailing along so beautifully, Lord, and
I'm thinking I'm a pretty good Christian woman
and mom—then along comes Aunt Gertrude.
Honestly, she is a barrel of terrible and she rolls
right over me! I guess everybody has an Aunt
Gertrude in their lives. No matter how hard it is,
I will trust You are working out our relationship
for good. Perhaps I am to learn the lesson of
humility. Or I'm to rely on Your divine patience
and discover the art of loving the unlovable. Or
maybe You want me to pray for Aunt Gertrude.
Thank You for Your gentle reminder to love those
who seem to be my enemies and persecute me.
And may my children see their mother taking
all her cares—even Aunt Gertrude—to You, Lord.
Amen.

THINK ABOUT IT:
Do you have someone in your life who is like Aunt
Gertrude? If so, how do you deal with the strife?
What is God teaching you in this situation?

I LOVE STUFF

When you ask, you do not receive, because you ask with wrong motives, that you may spend what you get on your pleasures.

JAMES 4:3

I love stuff, Lord. Doesn't everybody? We're told by some very knowledgeable advertising folks that we won't live well without a certain quantity of merchandise. Of course, later that same stuff ends up on a high shelf so I can't see the mental stamp of SILLY all over it. Maybe the reason some of my prayers don't get answered the way I hope is because my motives aren't always right. That is, I'm too busy asking for more stuff for my own pleasure. My children are watching me! Help me, Lord, to bring my prayer life into alignment with Your will, not mine. And allow my children to learn this important lesson—that sometimes we don't get what we ask for because we're asking with the wrong motives—along with me. Amen.

THINK ABOUT IT:

Do you have the right motives when you pray? If not, how can you improve with the Lord's help?

A SPIRITUAL LIFELINE

*One of those days Jesus went out to
a mountainside to pray, and spent
the night praying to God.*

LUKE 6:12

Lord, when I read about Your prayer life while You were on this earth, I'm deeply humbled. You spent a great deal of time in fellowship with the Father. Modern-day men and women tend to think of prayers in minutes or even seconds, hence the term, "breathing a prayer." Then we're off and running again with our hectic schedules. But You made prayer a fundamental part of Your life. May I always take the time for prayer, whatever amount of time it takes for fellowship, guidance, support, requests, encouragement, repentance, thanksgiving, and praise. May I, as well as my family, see prayer not as a quick fix, but as a spiritual lifeline—to You. Amen.

THINK ABOUT IT:
What prayers do you put off because you're too short on time? What can you do to strengthen prayer as your spiritual lifeline?

HOW I WANT TO LIVE

*"Watch and pray so that you will
not fall into temptation. The spirit
is willing, but the flesh is weak."*

MATTHEW 26:41

When it comes to temptation, Lord, many people aren't worried about it—they just give in to it! But I have also seen those same people as they deal with the aftermath of their choices. Not good. Sometimes there would be a season of elation and amusement as they gave in to sin, but when it was over, some kind of injury, grief, or destruction followed in its wake. That is not how I want to live my life, Lord, nor how I want my family to live. When we are enticed by temptations—no matter what kind—may we learn to rush to You in prayer and allow You to give us the courage and strength to flee from them! Amen.

THINK ABOUT IT:
What temptations have been enticing to you? Have you asked God to help you overcome those temptations?

FALLING INTO PLACE

*Jesus replied: " 'Love the Lord your God
with all your heart and with all your soul
and with all your mind.' This is the first
and greatest commandment."*

MATTHEW 22:37-38

When I read the above verses, Lord, I see how
simple our relationship really can be. Simple and
beautiful. It's easy for me to buy into the idea that
our relationship is complicated and unattainable
when considering all the opposing opinions and
theologies out there. But I understand these
verses so well, since they go right to the heart of
our father-daughter bond. If I love You—*really*
love You—then I wouldn't want to do anything to
harm our intimate fellowship. Everything would
fall into place, just as it was supposed to in the
Garden of Eden. What verses. Simply beautiful!
Amen.

THINK ABOUT IT:
Do you love God with all your heart and soul and
mind?

NOT THE END OF THE STORY

But mark this: There will be terrible times in the last days. People will be lovers of themselves, lovers of money, boastful, proud, abusive, disobedient to their parents, ungrateful, unholy, without love, unforgiving, slanderous, without self-control, brutal, not lovers of the good, treacherous, rash, conceited, lovers of pleasure rather than lovers of God—having a form of godliness but denying its power. Have nothing to do with such people.

2 TIMOTHY 3:1–5

Lord, I know You are returning, and we may be living in the last days, so help me to always be watchful and ready for You whenever that day of Your second coming may be. Please don't let me be swayed by people who are described in the verses above. May I train up my children so they will want to become lovers of You and not lovers of the world! Amen.

THINK ABOUT IT:
Are you and your family ready for the Lord's return?

LOVE SONGS

The Lord appeared to us in the past, saying:
"I have loved you with an everlasting love;
I have drawn you with unfailing kindness."

JEREMIAH 31:3

People love tender love stories and love songs because they show just how deeply and passionately the human heart can be touched. Perhaps in the verse above we see a bit of a love song, sung to Israel, but also sung to me, to my family, and all of mankind. May I always share Your Word with my children, Lord, so that they might know how You draw them near with unfailing kindness and how You love them with a love that is never ending. May their hearts embrace Your tender kindness and love always! In Jesus' name I pray. Amen.

THINK ABOUT IT:
Do your children know just how much God loves them? What are some ways to share that good news?

A HOT MESS OF WORRY!

Do not be anxious about anything, but in every situation, by prayer and petition, with thanksgiving, present your requests to God.

PHILIPPIANS 4:6

From a very young age, Lord, we learn to worry about our troubles. But then we read in Your Word that though there will be trouble in this life, we *shouldn't* worry (John 16:33). Since this means *no one* will escape tests and trials, how can I stay calm? Especially now that I have children—wee ones who never stop running headlong into peril—my ability to imagine what can go wrong at any given moment has skyrocketed! And, given that we live in a world that is getting darker spiritually, I've become a hot mess of worry! Yet, again, Your Word says we're to be anxious for nothing. And by that You mean absolutely *nothing*. Please show me, Lord, how I can live that way. I need Your divine help right now. In Jesus' name I pray. Amen.

THINK ABOUT IT:
What are a few worries you can bring before God right now?

ANOTHER GIFT FROM GOD

*Then God blessed the seventh day and made
it holy, because on it he rested from all the
work of creating that he had done.*

GENESIS 2:3

Lord, I confess that I've used most of my Sundays
to get caught up on all the miscellaneous "other
work" that I couldn't get done during the week,
and in doing so, I've only made myself even more
bleary-eyed tired. Because Sunday was made for
man, not the other way around, Lord, I know You
mean for this special day to be given to us not
as an impossible rule to follow, but as a gift to
receive. It's to be a wonderful refreshment for our
bodies, minds, and spirits. Please help me and
my family learn how to use our Sundays as You
see fit, so together we can start the new week
with eagerness and joy! Amen.

THINK ABOUT IT:
What are some ways you can rest on Sunday and
be refreshed for the new week? If you can't rest
on a Sunday, on what day can you be refreshed?

MAKE ME READY FOR MORE

I gave you milk, not solid food,
for you were not yet ready for it.
Indeed, you are still not ready.

1 CORINTHIANS 3:2

Lord, I want to grow spiritually. I sense that my soul has been stuck in a rut for a long time. Maybe it's because I didn't want to change. After all, change can be scary! But I want to please You in all I do, so give me courage to become the woman, wife, and mother You created me to be. Even if the process is painful, help me to be open to moving beyond the baby-milk phase, and make me ready for solid spiritual food. I'm excited about a deeper understanding of Your Word, growing up as a Christian, and a closer relationship with You! In Jesus' name I pray. Amen.

THINK ABOUT IT:

What are some of the ways you can know you're moving beyond the milk phase as a Christian?

NOT LEFT BEHIND

*"I will not leave you as orphans;
I will come to you."*

JOHN 14:18

Jesus, I'm sitting here in the night, awake again—but this time it's not because of my baby's crying or because I have to go to the bathroom for the eighteenth time. I'm just awake, thinking about this little life You have placed in my hands, and I feel so unworthy, so in awe, so alone. But You have promised that You will come, so I know You are here, even now in this darkness. Even here in this mess of a nursery, rocking back and forth with me, breathing in, breathing out. Your Spirit comforts me, Jesus, like the soothing of a mother's hand on a baby's warm back. Thank You, Lord. I'll keep breathing and rocking and depending on You. Amen.

THINK ABOUT IT:
Do you live as if you fully believe Jesus is with you in every moment? If not, what can you do to breathe Him into your life?

POWER IN FRAGILITY

*But we have this treasure in jars of clay
to show that this all-surpassing power
is from God and not from us.*

2 CORINTHIANS 4:7

Lord, have mercy on me. You must know I'm feeling pretty cracked today. Nothing's gone right. I can't seem to say a right word, think a clear thought, or give a good direction. Your wisdom escapes me, and when I grasp for answers, it all just comes out sounding like nonsense. My children aren't listening—I believe they may think Mom's really gone off the deep end this time. But yet, I know they know Your truth. I know they see Your light. Somehow, God, I've managed to teach them to trust You—even when my tongue has failed me. Thank You for shining through this broken vessel. Thank You for Your power that is greater than my performance. Amen.

THINK ABOUT IT:
When do you feel God's power the most?

MARVELOUS

*For you are great and do marvelous
deeds; you alone are God.*

PSALM 86:10

God, Your work is marvelous. There is no end to
the goodness You have put into this child of mine.
I count the small yet perfectly formed toes and
am amazed at Your attention to detail. From the
soft, wispy hair to the squishy elbow dimples, to
the wrinkly soles, this baby has Your fingerprints
all over. I want to know what You whisper into
that sweet ear that makes a smile appear. What
warm breeze do You blow on those eyelids that
cause them to flutter and open, revealing sparkling
eyes full of wonder? What song are You singing
that causes my baby to gurgle and coo and hum
along? I'm so thankful for this child. I'm so glad
for Your work, Lord. In my baby, and in me. Amen.

THINK ABOUT IT:
What everyday wonders can you thank God for
today?

WHEN I'VE LOST IT

*The one who has knowledge uses
words with restraint, and whoever
has understanding is even-tempered.*

PROVERBS 17:27

I've done it again, Lord. My children are walking on eggshells around me. Trying to be so perfect and quiet. Trying to...well...not be children. I've messed up. I let my temper get the best of me. I let the anger and frustration bubble up inside me. I forgot to take a breath. I forgot to take a walk. I need to go slowly. I don't have to lose it just because the glass of bright red juice has spilled on the snow-white carpet. Who needs white carpet anyway? Lord, You spilled Your bright red blood to make my soul like a white clean floor. Surely whatever troubles come today are covered by You. And so I accept Your grace for my anger. And I'll ask forgiveness from my children. Please let them see Your grace in me. Amen.

THINK ABOUT IT:
In what ways do you need to have more restraint? What do you think your children learn about you, your faith, and your God when you apologize?

LOVE HURTS

Have mercy on me, L<small>ORD</small>, for I am faint;
heal me, L<small>ORD</small>, for my bones are in
agony. My soul is in deep anguish.
How long, L<small>ORD</small>, how long?

P<small>SALM</small> 6:2–3

Oh God, it hurts so much to love people sometimes. I give so much, care so much, and it takes so much out of me. Lord, my heart is breaking for my dear ones. They are aching, and I am aching. They are in turmoil, and I am in turmoil. I haven't caused this pain. No one has. But still, it's there. As real and as sickening as a punch in the gut. Sometimes when I think about it, I can't even breathe. "My bones are in agony. My soul is in deep anguish." But Lord, You know this kind of pain. You know every inch of the hurt we are feeling. You know what it's like to hurt for the ones You love. God, help me get through this. Help me be strong for my loves. Amen.

THINK ABOUT IT:
What good can come through hurting for others? How can you increase your God-given strength during those times?

THAT MOM

The wise woman builds her house, but with her own hands the foolish one tears hers down.

PROVERBS 14:1

God, the teenagers are getting to me. They've got these rolling eyes and smirks and snappy replies, and some days, to be honest, I just can't deal with them. Lord, help me not to be "that mom." Help me not be a nagging, complaining, or whining voice but a strong, calm, and wise voice in their lives. Help me firmly plant myself as part of their foundation—not their friend, not their fellow wanderer, but their solid ground and intelligent guide. And, Lord, please, in the name of all that is good and holy, let me somehow steer them clear of all the stupid mistakes I made when I was their age! Amen.

THINK ABOUT IT:
How can you remind yourself to have patience with your kids? What are some verses that will help you and your children keep your feet on God's pathway?

MOTHER WARRIOR

"The LORD will fight for you;
you need only to be still."

EXODUS 14:14

God, my mother-warrior fire rose up in me today.
I want to run in and fight my child's battles, slay
the dragons, and save the day. I want to take over,
take the offender down, and take control. But then
I realize that even if I could do all those things,
it wouldn't necessarily be the best thing. And
sometimes I just have to let my kid fight those
battles—all alone. But not really all alone, right,
Lord? Please help me remember You are always
there, and You make a better warrior, protector,
and deliverer than I could ever be. Amen.

THINK ABOUT IT:
How do you decide when to step in and when to let
your child fight battles on his or her own? When
will you claim Exodus 14:14 as your very own?

DR. MOM

*"To God belong wisdom and power;
counsel and understanding are his."*

JOB 12:13

Lord, healer and provider, I ask You to heal my child today. I feel as though sometimes moms need a medical degree to help their kids survive childhood—so many mysterious sniffles, coughs, rashes, and rattles. It's so hard to know what to do—when to take them to the doctor and when not to. What guidance to follow. What advice to take. Whom to trust. So I just try to do my best. And now I place my child in Your hands. For there, all our children can be safe and secure. I ask You to make it clear to me what I need to know. And help me be patient about the things I don't. Amen.

THINK ABOUT IT:
What worry about your child do you need to bring to God today?

HURTFUL WORDS, HEALING WORDS

The words of the reckless pierce like swords,
but the tongue of the wise brings healing.

PROVERBS 12:18

Lord, I am trying to keep my cool. Really, I am. But someone has said something unkind about my child. And *I* felt the sting of the jab directed at my little one. Words can be so hurtful. And I can't explain to him why this has happened. Because there's no reason for it. People are just mean sometimes. That's what I told him. But that isn't a good enough reason for him, Lord, nor for me either. What else can I say? Hm. Now, when I stop and think about it, I realize You know exactly what it feels like to have people mock and ridicule Your very own Son. Yes, Father, You really do. Forgiveness? Yes, Lord. I'll try that. Grace? Yes, Lord, I'll take that too. Your wise, healing words for me to pass on to my little one? Please, yes, and thank You. Amen.

THINK ABOUT IT:
What do you do when someone is unkind to you or your child? What verses can you memorize that are sure to bring healing into these kinds of situations?

STUMPED

"I will lead the blind by the ways they have not known, along unfamiliar paths I will guide them; I will turn the darkness into light before them and make the rough places smooth."

ISAIAH 42:16

Wow. I mean, really, wow. I'm stumped, Lord. This kid has got me tied up in so many knots, I don't even know where my ends are. Every time I think I've got this parenting thing all figured out, it turns out I don't. The dog dies, the homework disappears, the kid cries uncontrollably because the peanut butter is smooth instead of crunchy, and so on. Why didn't You tell me this would be so hard? You did? Well, You were right. But I wouldn't have it any other way. Help me, Lord, to see the best next step to take. But first, maybe You could show me where my left shoe is? Because I can't seem to find it anywhere. . . Amen.

THINK ABOUT IT:
What has stumped you about your kid lately? Have you prayed about it? If so, how might God already be helping you?

PERFECT MOMMIES

I trust in you; do not let me be put to shame,
nor let my enemies triumph over me.

Psalm 25:2

Oh, great. Lord, help me. I'm sitting here in my car, and I see them. The perfect mommies. The ones with the fifty-dollar hairdos and spray-on tans and frozen smiles. And I don't even want to move, Lord. I really don't. Can I just stay in here? And avoid their stares when they see my ratty ball cap covering my unwashed hair, and my varicose-veined legs, and, why yes, that *is* spit-up on my shirt. Father, I am a hot mess. And yet You still look at me and tell me I'm beautiful. Okay, Lord, I'll get out of the car. I will go pick up my kid. And I will hold my head up high—and maybe then they won't notice that I have my fuzzy slippers on. Amen.

THINK ABOUT IT:
What's your attitude about mommy judgment? How can God help you from judging those who seem like perfect mommies?

ANXIETY TEST

Search me, God, and know my heart;
test me and know my anxious thoughts.

PSALM 139:23

It's all right, isn't it, God? You're a father—You're the Father of us all. You must have known this feeling more than once. When one of Your children wants to go a different way. When she wants to just go away—far away. I know I've done all I can to teach her well. I know she has a good head on her shoulders. And I know You will go with her. Yet even knowing all of that, I'm still afraid, Lord. I am worried. God, help me to admit that to You. Help me to tell her that I love her and I trust her, but that I'm concerned for her too. And, God? Replace my fear and worry with courage and peace as I learn to trust in You more. Amen.

THINK ABOUT IT:
What helps you feel less anxious for your child? What Bible verses can you plant in your heart to keep the worries and fears at bay?

NOT THE OLD DAYS ANYMORE

Do not say, "Why were the old days better than these?" For it is not wise to ask such questions.
ECCLESIASTES 7:10

God, I used to do so many things. I used to have hobbies, read books, and do crafts. I used to go out with friends, have dinner parties, and go on spur-of-the-moment trips. There is so much of me that I don't recognize anymore, Lord. Much of my life has become so routine, so scheduled, and so full of things I do for other people. They are my people. And I love them, God. But sometimes I wonder if I've gotten a little lost in the middle of it all. Sometimes I feel a little bit sad about losing part of who I am. Lord, can You help me find a better balance? Can You help me find me? Amen.

THINK ABOUT IT:
What can you do to find a better balance between life as a mom and the rest of who you are—in God's eyes and your own?

WHEN I NEED UNDERSTANDING

Great is our Lord and mighty in power;
his understanding has no limit.

PSALM 147:5

Lord, I need Your clarity. I need Your understanding. I need the wisdom of Solomon and the patience of Job. I need to be able to explain things clearly. I need to have courage to face my own fears about this. And I need to have the determination to stick to it, even when things get tricky. Because I know things will get hard, Lord. I just know there will come a time when one or both of us want to chuck it all out the window and go get ice cream. But I also know that with You, we can do this. Together, we can get it done. I mean, it's just seventh-grade math, right? Amen.

THINK ABOUT IT:
What's something hard that you have faced for your child's benefit? How did God and His Word help you?

FORMED IN THE WOMB

*"This is what the L*ORD* says—your Redeemer,
who formed you in the womb: I am the L*ORD*,
the Maker of all things."*

ISAIAH 44:24

God of all creation, I am standing here in awe of Your accomplishments. I look at these children and see the amazing way You have created every inch of us to fit together perfectly. You have formed these organs, tissues, and systems that all depend on each other and are shaped to work with efficiency, strength, and power. And at every stage of growth, I become more astounded by Your plan for us, Lord. How did You do it? How do You keep making, creating, forming, and producing? And how do You do it so beautifully, Lord? I may never know or understand how, but I thank You—for paying attention to every detail and for these little wonders You have entrusted to me. Amen.

THINK ABOUT IT:
What's something about the human body that you find amazing? Why not praise God for it right now?

WHEN I NEED REFRESHING

"I will refresh the weary and satisfy the faint."
JEREMIAH 31:25

God, my joints ache. My feet hurt. My head is spinning. My heart is pumping so hard, I can almost feel the pressure inside my arteries. I can't seem to get a good breath. And there are sore muscles where I didn't even know I had muscles. God, this is some kind of crazy workout routine, do You know that? Every day I realize just a bit more how little I understood about parenting before now. And every day I become a little bit more grateful for what my parents did for me. Keeping up with a house of toddlers is serious business, Lord. And I honestly don't know if I can physically do it! Help me, almighty God. Help me keep going. One. More. Day. Amen.

THINK ABOUT IT:
How has becoming a mother challenged you physically? What can you do to tap into the strength of God's Spirit?

TOUGH DECISIONS

Give careful thought to the paths for your
feet and be steadfast in all your ways.

PROVERBS 4:26

God, it's time. I have been dreading this day and this decision. But now it's here. And I want so much to be doing the right thing, Lord. I have prayed and prayed about this. You know how often I have come before You and laid this struggle at Your feet. And yet still, a voice of doubt creeps into my head. Lord, I ask You one more time—if this is the right thing to do for my family, please let me know that. Please let me feel Your peace. And if, even after all this time, I've got it wrong, then please let me know that too. Let Your will be done. And let me see it clearly. Amen.

THINK ABOUT IT:

What's your process for making tough decisions? How easy is it for you to leave the results in God's hands?

WHEN I FEEL ABANDONED

"Do not be afraid; do not be discouraged, for the LORD your God will be with you wherever you go."
JOSHUA 1:9

God, I feel so disappointed. When I knew I would soon have a family of my own, I had all these dreams about what that would look like. And the members of my own family—the one I grew up in—were always part of that picture. I thought they would help me, support me, and be there for me. But now I feel they have abandoned me. They don't seem to care that much about being involved in my life or in the life of my child. Lord, help me to see the truth in this situation. And help me to express how I feel in ways that will be helpful. I am hurt and confused. But I don't want to hurt anyone else. Amen.

THINK ABOUT IT:
What do you do when people let you down? How wonderful is it knowing God will never disappoint or leave you?

ENOUGH TROUBLE

*"Do not worry about tomorrow,
for tomorrow will worry about itself.
Each day has enough trouble of its own."*

MATTHEW 6:34

Lord, can I please have a few more hours in the day? I know that's a lot to ask. It seems like an impossible request. Yet I myself feel like I am constantly being asked to do the impossible. How in the world am I supposed to pick up one kid from practice and attend the concert of another on the other side of town at the same time? How am I supposed to feed my family and pets, fill the prescriptions, iron the uniforms, and help with the littlest one's book report? How am I supposed to remember to wash the dog and walk the laundry? There just isn't enough time, Lord. There isn't enough *me*. Help me do what I can and be content with that. Amen.

THINK ABOUT IT:
What do you do when you feel stretched? What Bible verse can you cling to for relief?

LEARNING THE SECRET

I have learned the secret of being content in any and every situation, whether well fed or hungry, whether living in plenty or in want.

PHILIPPIANS 4:12

God, I'm looking under the couch cushions, in the bottom of my purse, and in the pockets of my husband's jeans—but it's just no use. Although I have found a lost foam dart, my missing earring, and a solitary piece of gum, I cannot find enough money to pay for all the things my children want this month. Sports gear, new shoes, tickets to the school play, and admission for the field trip—I just can't afford it all. But what do I cut out? And which kid do I disappoint? God, help me to show my children that sometimes life means making hard choices. And sometimes we don't get to do or have everything we want. And that's okay. Help me to be okay in admitting that, Lord. Amen.

THINK ABOUT IT:
How do you handle living on a budget? How comforting is it knowing that in this, as in all things, God has a plan for you and your family?

WHEN I NEED MY FRIENDS

*A friend loves at all times, and a
brother is born for a time of adversity.*
PROVERBS 17:17

God, I know they are around here somewhere.
They used to be here all the time. They were
such a huge part of my life once. There was a
time when I didn't go a day, or sometimes even
an hour, without them. But now, Lord? Where
are they now? It seems like ever since I had kids,
my old friends have disappeared. They have lives
of their own. I totally understand that. And, yes,
there were many times I had to turn them down—
times when I just couldn't go out. I couldn't leave
my kids. So why do I feel so neglected and left
out? Lord, help me to reconnect with the people
I care about. Help me to make the time and find
the energy to cultivate good, healthy relationships, Lord. I need some friends. Amen.

THINK ABOUT IT:
What can you do to stay in touch with your
friends? What do you do to stay in touch with
your friend Jesus?

ON BECOMING MY MOTHER

Start children off on the way they should go,
and even when they are old
they will not turn from it.

Proverbs 22:6

Oh no, Lord. I don't know where that voice came from. But I have definitely heard it before. What did I just say? I can't believe I actually said *that* to my kids. I promised myself I would never say such things. I told my husband I'd never do it—that on no account, for no reason, in no way would I ever, ever, ever do it. But here I am. And now I've done it. I've become my mother. And You know what, Lord? I have to say, it's not so bad. God, thank You for giving me a parent who really cared for me and loved me enough to tell me not to run with scissors, make my face freeze that way, or heat the whole neighborhood. Thank You for the lessons I received about starving children in Africa and how anything worth doing is worth doing well. Thank You, Lord, for mothers. Amen.

THINK ABOUT IT:
What lessons did your mother repeat often? What lessons do you hear God repeating to you often?

LAUGH ALONG

"He will yet fill your mouth with laughter
and your lips with shouts of joy."

JOB 8:21

God, their giggles are like gold. Their laughter is like a summer breeze. Their joy is like the greatest treasure I could ever find. Thank You, Lord, for happy children. Thank You for how much they make me laugh. Thank You for their silly jokes and unexpected pranks. Thank You for their witty replies and silly antics. Thank You for their tumbles and bumbles. Thank You for shy smiles and red cheeks. Thank You for all the mistakes we have been able to make and chuckle about together. Thank You for these beautiful moments when I get just a glimpse of the everlasting lightness that we will someday live in every minute together. Amen.

THINK ABOUT IT:
How do you feel when you hear your children laughing? How do you think God feels when He hears *you* laughing?

BREAKTHROUGHS

*Apply your heart to instruction and
your ears to words of knowledge.*

PROVERBS 23:12

Lord, I want to just take a breath and savor this moment. To see my child's eyes light up with understanding—to see him in that *aha* moment—is just about the most rewarding few seconds of my life. Thank You for breakthroughs, Lord. Thank You for giving us brains that click and can form connections between all the bits of information we are taking in all the time. Thank You for encouraging me to keep trying. And thank You for letting me witness this one brief flash of knowledge gained and explored for the first time. What an honor! Help me remember this time, Lord. Help me remember that this is reason enough to keep on teaching, training, and serving. The wonder of it all! Amen.

THINK ABOUT IT:
What breakthrough have you witnessed recently in your child's life? What breakthrough has God witnessed recently in your *own* life?

DIFFERENT

*He has made everything
beautiful in its time.*

ECCLESIASTES 3:11

God, I certainly know what it's like to feel like the ugly duckling. I remember so well the awkwardness of childhood. I remember feeling like my arms and legs had minds of their own. I remember thinking how much I didn't fit in—how I stood out in all the wrong ways. And I remember believing it was never going to get better. Help me have all those memories in my head when I talk to my child today. Help me have greater sympathy and the patience to just sit and listen. Help me give her some hope that things will change. And help me give her confidence in knowing that You and I agree she is beautiful. Amen.

THINK ABOUT IT:
What is a good thing about being different? How has God made *you* different, even now?

MY STRENGTH

The LORD is my strength and my shield;
my heart trusts in him, and he helps me.

PSALM 28:7

God, I know I'm supposed to be the strong one.
I'm supposed to hold us together. I'm supposed
to put on a brave face and act like I have it all
together. I'm supposed to have the answers. But
God, You know I don't. I just don't have it in me
today. And I feel so weak, uncertain, and afraid.
Lord, I am depending wholly on You. I place my
mouth, my mind, and my spirit in Your hands.
Give me words of comfort and hope. Grant me
clarity and peace. Fill me up with Your courage
and power. I have no idea how to get through this
day, Lord, but I know I can do it with You beside
me. Amen.

THINK ABOUT IT:
How do you feel when you are fully dependent
on God?

ALL DAY LONG

*The Israelites went up to her to
have their disputes decided.*

JUDGES 4:5

So many decisions, Lord. What time to leave, which route to take, what to pack, what to do when we get there. What to have for dinner, how to cook it, what seasonings will work, and how long to let it sit. Which socks go with what shirt, where the belt is, and who should shower first. Can these clothes be washed on warm? Is it *i* before *e* here or *e* before *i*? Is it okay to eat these leftovers? Where did the remote go? How long will it take us to get to the doctor's office? All day long. Every single day. One million decisions. A thousand arguments. I'm no Judge Deborah, Lord. I'm bound to get one or two things wrong. Help my family members to be gracious when I do. And help me to love them even if they aren't. Amen.

THINK ABOUT IT:
How do you cope with the stress of making daily decisions? How often do you ask God for advice?

NO WHITE FLAGS HERE

Watch your life and doctrine closely.
Persevere in them, because if you do,
you will save both yourself and your hearers.

1 TIMOTHY 4:16

God, sometimes I want to fly the white flag. I want to say enough is enough. I want to call it quits. I've tried this motherhood thing out, and I just am not good at it. I'm giving it my best shot—I promise! But these kids have just got me going in circles, and I don't know how to achieve any kind of success. I'm not even sure I would know success if it came up and slapped a blue ribbon right across my face. Heavenly Father, help me to gain just a bit of Your perspective. Help me to keep persevering, even on days like today, when it doesn't seem worth it. I don't really want to give up, Lord. I want to give it my all. Amen.

THINK ABOUT IT:
What do you do when you feel like giving up? How do you gain a God-perspective?

SING IT

*"The LORD your God is with you, the Mighty
Warrior who saves. He will take great delight
in you; in his love he will no longer rebuke you,
but will rejoice over you with singing."*

ZEPHANIAH 3:17

God, the dryer is buzzing, the alarm ringing, and
the skillet sizzling. My head is pounding and
the TV is almost drowning out the noise of the
kids sounding off on some subject they know
so little about. Now the bacon is burning, my
stomach churning, and my kid's face is turning
red. Meanwhile, the pop songs are bubbling, the
baby gurgling, and the trouble doubling as the
two older ones' voices rise. And this is the song
of my morning, Lord. This is the song of my life.
Lord, in all of this cacophony of sound and fury,
please let me hear the song You are singing for
me. Amen.

THINK ABOUT IT:
If you were to sing a new song for God, what
would it sound like?

TWINKLE

"Those who are wise will shine like the brightness of the heavens, and those who lead many to righteousness, like the stars for ever and ever."

"Twinkle, twinkle, my little stars. . ." God, help me show my children how proud I am of them. Help me tell them how pleased I am to be their mother. *"How I wonder what you are. . ."* I know I don't understand them very well at times. I'm constantly surprised by the things they are able to do. *"Up above the world so high. . ."* I want to help them to keep soaring, to keep reaching for their dreams. *"Like a diamond in the sky. . ."* I want them to keep shining for You, Lord. *"Twinkle, twinkle, my little stars. . ."* They seem so small, and yet they are growing so fast. *"How I wonder what you are."* I have so many hopes for them, Lord. Yet help me remember my hope always comes from You. Good night, and amen.

THINK ABOUT IT:
How does your life reflect your hope in God?

MY CHICKS

How priceless is your unfailing love, O God!
People take refuge in the shadow of your wings.

PSALM 36:7

I want to gather them up, Lord, and protect them—like little chicks under the hen's warm, strong wings. I want to keep them from physical harm; but more than that, I want to shield their minds from twisted messages that masquerade as truth. I want to keep them from seeing the darkness in the world. I want to save their hearts from being broken. But I know I can't keep them safe forever. They will have to go out and have experiences and try new things. They will have to make mistakes and learn from them and grow. They will have to test their beliefs and be tested. They will have to love, and sometimes they will have to lose. Lord, although I feel unprepared for all this, I know You will give me the strength when I need it. But maybe just for today, I'll cuddle my chicks a little bit longer. Amen.

THINK ABOUT IT:
How do you deal with giving freedom to your child? How does it feel knowing God will protect them?

GOOD NEWS

*Like cold water to a weary soul is
good news from a distant land.*

PROVERBS 25:25

Lord, today I cried at the mailbox. I freely admit it. I was so happy to have that piece of good news. I was so relieved to hear that something my child had wanted so much was actually going to happen. And I was just humbled by the thought of all the good-news messages You have brought us. I am so thankful for negative test results and good report cards; for paid bills and funded grants; for those messages of trips ended safely and feet on the ground; for accidents averted, traffic avoided, and storms that missed us by miles; for every little and big thing You've done for me. And I'm so thankful for the best "good news" of all—Your Son. Amen.

THINK ABOUT IT:

What good-news story have you heard recently? Have you thanked God for it?

WITNESSES

*Since we are surrounded by such a great cloud
of witnesses, let us throw off everything that
hinders and the sin that so easily entangles.*

HEBREWS 12:1

Lord, this is a big day in my child's life. And I
hope she feels the weight of it. I want her to know
that today she is making a choice that has been
made by millions of others through hundreds
and thousands of years. Today she is standing
in the sandals of Abraham when he heard Your
promise and followed You. She is walking on
the path of Moses as he led the people through
the wilderness. She is taking the steps of Peter
as he strode out upon the water. She is laying
down her will for Yours, as did Mary, knowing
nothing is impossible with You. Lord, thank You
for Your salvation. Thank You for Your gift of
grace. And thank You today for giving the best
present to my child. Amen.

THINK ABOUT IT:
How can you support your child's decision to grow
in faith? How do you support your own?

FIRSTS

"Speak, for your servant is listening."

1 Samuel 3:10

Oh Lord! What a beautiful sound! I can't get over my own amazement at something so simple. But in that one second it took for my child to utter a word—an intelligible, clear group of familiar sounds—worlds changed. I know other words will soon come. In a trickle at first, and then one day a whole river of vocabulary, gushing out from my child's sweet little mouth. I'm sure that someday soon—maybe even sooner than I think—I might get tired of hearing this sound. But for today, it is a wonder. Today, it is a great achievement. Today, my child and I stepped one little bit closer to understanding each other. And right now, the sweetest sound in the world is "Mama." Thank You, Lord, for words! Amen.

THINK ABOUT IT:

What does it mean to you to hear your child speak? When was the last time your Father God heard you call Him "Abba"?

HELP IS ON THE WAY

*"I will talk to the Father, and he'll provide
you another Friend so that you will
always have someone with you."*

JOHN 14:16 MSG

God, You know how much I want to be a helper. Someone I know is in trouble and I want more than anything to drop all my plans, reach out my two hands, and lift up my friend. But I can't. My plans are not my own. My day is wrapped up in my children's needs and wants. And they are things that just can't be postponed. Not now. So, Lord, my prayer is that You send someone to help my friend. Someone to fill my shoes and take my place. Someone to give her everything she needs. And, Lord, if there's anything else I can do, please show me. Amen.

THINK ABOUT IT:
What things can you do to help someone when you can't be physically present? How does God help you without Him being physically present?

TOGETHER

Teach [my words] to your children,
talking about them when you sit at home
and when you walk along the road,
when you lie down and when you get up.

DEUTERONOMY 11:19

Lord, he wants things one way. I want them another. Sometimes I don't understand how a man I live with every day could be such a stranger to me. And this time, Lord, we are disagreeing about how to parent our children. It means so much to me that we get on the same page and present a clear message to our kids. But how can we do that when we can't even hear each other speak? Lord, I know I share the responsibility of this. I know I've been wrong—trying too hard to get a word in instead of listening. God, help us to work this out together. To stand strong together. To be good parents *together*. Amen.

THINK ABOUT IT:
Why not ask God what you can do to parent better together?

FAITHFUL PROMISES

The LORD is trustworthy in all he promises and faithful in all he does.

PSALM 145:13

The chubby cheeks fill up and blow on the fuzzy dandelion head, and the seeds fly, floating on the breeze, settling on the lawn, tumbling on a wave of air into the distance. And as the seeds drift away, I think of every promise You have given us. Promises to love and take care of us. Promises to watch over us. Promises never to leave us. And each promise of Yours is like a seed in our lives, planting us into Your foundation, and giving us hope to grow on. Lord, may my child always know Your promises. May I teach them every day through the way I live for You. Amen.

THINK ABOUT IT:
What is one of God's promises that you are counting on?

WHEN I'M AFRAID

*"What is the matter, Hagar? Do not be afraid;
God has heard the boy crying as he lies there."*

GENESIS 21:17

Lord, oh how we prayed for this child. And now, when I'm waiting here on this strange bed, I'm filled with fear. There are beeps and signals and sounds of alarm. There are whirring machines and spinning wheels and creaky chairs. And I must rest, but I can't. Lord, be with the doctors who are holding my child now. Let their skilled hands find anything that is out of place. Let their knowledgeable eyes search the tiny body and see all that You see, Lord. And let them love my child. I know they are strangers; they are not family, God. But let them love my child, and let my small baby feel their love. And let me love them in return. Amen.

THINK ABOUT IT:
Have you ever feared for your child's safety? How did you cope with that? How does it help knowing God sees and hears all?

PONDERING

*Mary treasured up all these things
and pondered them in her heart.*

LUKE 2:19

Sweet baby Jesus, what did You hear when Your young mother first held You in her arms? What song did she sing to calm Your cries? And what did You feel as she wrapped the cloth around You? Did You feel warm and safe in her arms? Jesus, I know Your mother loved You. Oh, how she loved You! She risked so much just to let You be born into this world. She took on so much responsibility. She trusted in Your Father, even when she didn't fully understand. Sweet baby Jesus, thank You for coming to us. I am forever grateful. I will forever treasure You. Amen.

THINK ABOUT IT:
What must it have felt like to hold the infant Jesus?

SAFE PLACE

*"In your unfailing love you will lead the people
you have redeemed. In your strength you will
guide them to your holy dwelling."*

ExODUS 15:13

I look into my child's eyes, and I see my own. I
listen to his words and hear my thoughts. I walk
with him and see my stride. Lord, there is so much
of me in him, and so much of him in me. God, as
he grows and changes and becomes older and
more mature, I pray one thing. Let him always
be happy to come home. Let him always feel
safe here with me. Let him always be confident
that if he comes to me with a secret, a trouble, or
a sadness, I will listen and try to make it better.
And let him always be absolutely, positively sure
of my love, as I am sure of Yours. Amen.

THINK ABOUT IT:
When do you feel most secure? What Bible verse
makes you feel snug in God's arms?

SPECIAL BLESSINGS

Thanks be to God for his indescribable gift!
2 CORINTHIANS 9:15

Lord, there has not been a single day, not a minute, that has gone by that I have not been thankful for having this child of mine. Sometimes I think people feel sorry for me. Or maybe they want me to feel sorry. But I don't. They take one look at him and put him in a category—label him as "less." But I look at him and only see more and more and more. More joy. More smiles. More unconditional love. God, You have taught me so much through this child! You have taught me patience, trust, and courage. I will never stop thanking You for this gift. I will never stop reveling in the blessings I have through my special child. Amen.

THINK ABOUT IT:
What comfort comes through assigning labels or categories to people? What harm comes? What can you do to see all people through *God's* eyes?

JUST A MOM

*We do not belong to those who shrink
back and are destroyed, but to those
who have faith and are saved.*

HEBREWS 10:39

Dear Lord, sometimes I feel like my voice is silenced. Like I don't get as much attention, as much power, or as much of a vote in issues that are important to me. I'm not a professional. I'm not a doctor or a lawyer, though I could have been. I've made different choices in my life, it's true. But I have a brain, and I have some valid things to say. Help me know when You want me to speak out, Lord, and when You want me to be silent. Help me not be afraid to speak because I'm "just a mom." Moms think. Moms do. And moms work hard! Help me to remember to look for opportunities to talk to others about You. Amen.

THINK ABOUT IT:

What is one issue in your community where your involvement might make a difference? What might God be leading you to do—or say?

SMALL VICTORIES

*"Do not despise these small beginnings,
for the LORD rejoices to see the work begin."*

ZECHARIAH 4:10 NLT

Lord of the universe, I didn't make any worlds today or move any mountains (unless you count a mountain of wet towels and dirty socks). I didn't save any souls or even make much of a sacrifice (unless you count letting my daughter in the shower first). But here's what I did do. I managed to get out of bed on time, even though *someone* woke me up three times in the night because "dinosaurs are in my underwear drawer." I delivered breakfast to the table and packed lunches. I shoved kids out the door and on to the bus. And at the grocery, I performed the miracle of multiplication and somehow stretched fifty bucks into twice that (with the blessing of coupons). I know it may not seem like much, Lord. But I'm rejoicing anyway. And I'm thankful for every little thing. Amen.

THINK ABOUT IT:
What small victories have you experienced today? Do you feel God rejoicing with you?

A PRAYER FOR LEADERS

*Encourage one another and build each other up,
just as in fact you are doing. Now we ask you,
brothers and sisters, to acknowledge those who
work hard among you, who care for you in the
Lord and who admonish you.*

1 THESSALONIANS 5:11–12

Holy God, today I want to remember those who are leading in our church. Sometimes it must be hard to care for our brothers and sisters in Christ. There are so many different personalities, troubles, backgrounds, and baggage. People in the church have human emotions and needs, just like everyone else. And it must be so stressful to hear so many stories and not always be able to fix the problems. On top of that, the church leaders are the target for so much criticism, both from within the church and beyond. Lord, help me be a voice of encouragement and a comfort to those who are leading. Amen.

THINK ABOUT IT:
What might God be prompting you to do to encourage and lift up your community's pastors and leaders today?

SLUMBER

He will not let your foot slip—he who watches over you will not slumber.

PSALM 121:3

Lord, have mercy. I. Need. Sleep. Night after night, I have been jolted out of bed by a child's cry, a creaky step, or nature's call. I think those last five pounds I gained must all be in my eyelids. I drink cup after cup of coffee, and it doesn't even make a dent in the fatigue. I am so thankful, Lord, that *You* don't require sleep. I'm so grateful that I can rest in the peace that comes from knowing You are always looking out for me. But, Lord, I most certainly do need sleep. Could You please give me just five more minutes of it? Or maybe five more days? Hey—it's really quiet here right now. No one's around. And the dishes can wait. Thanks, Lord! I'll just be going. . .amen.

THINK ABOUT IT:
What changes can you make to help you get the sleep you need? How does it feel knowing God will watch over you whenever you do catch some z's?

BEAUTY

Your beauty should not come from outward adornment, such as elaborate hairstyles and the wearing of gold jewelry or fine clothes. Rather, it should be that of your inner self, the unfading beauty of a gentle and quiet spirit, which is of great worth in God's sight.

1 PETER 3:3-4

God, I look in the mirror, and I wish I could see myself like You see me. I see the shadows under my eyes, the frowny forehead, and the five pimples that have shown up to the party. I don't see beauty. But then I think about how I kissed my beautiful daughter's face this morning. And I remember smelling the top of my handsome son's head. All that beauty has come from me and is being nurtured by me. And I think if all of that is somehow growing because of me, even a little bit, then somewhere that beauty is inside me too. Thank You, Lord, for helping me feel beautiful. Amen.

THINK ABOUT IT:
What is beautiful in your life? What steps can you take to increase your own inner beauty, the beauty God really values?

FREE REIN

*"I loathe my very life; therefore I will give
free rein to my complaint and speak
out in the bitterness of my soul."*

JOB 10:1

My Father God, You amaze me. I can't stand to hear my kid whining for even ten seconds, and yet You have listened to years of my complaints, and the complaints of millions and millions of others like me. Most of us have nothing to compare to Job's list of grievances. Yet we come to You with our headaches, our office conflicts, and our high water bills. We come day after day, and You listen, hour after hour. You invite us to come to You. Your patience with us is so tender. And Your wisdom that You guide us with always seems to fit every need. Lord, how You love us! Thank You! Amen.

THINK ABOUT IT:
What are you wanting to complain about most right now? What wisdom from God might remedy that complaint?

NO COMPARISON

With whom, then, will you compare God?
To what image will you liken him?
ISAIAH 40:18

So many screens, Lord. My life is filled with screens. TV screens, phone screens, tablet screens, and computer screens. And they all seem to be screaming for my attention. *Look at me! Be distracted! Waste your time!* Lord, I want my eyes to be on You. I want my mind to be filled with Your Word. I want my heart to be fully devoted to You. Help me, Lord. Help me block out all the distractions that are nothing, *absolutely nothing,* compared to the life You have planned for me. There is no image, no item, no video, no article that can benefit me as much as spending more time with You. Help me to be a good example for my children. Help me to show them what it looks like to focus on You. Amen.

THINK ABOUT IT:
What is distracting you lately? What small routine can you incorporate into your life to increase your God-focus?

DECIDED LONG AGO

Long before he laid down earth's foundations,
he had us in mind, had settled on us as the focus
of his love, to be made whole and holy by his
love. Long, long ago he decided to adopt us
into his family through Jesus Christ.

Ephesians 1:4–5 msg

Father in heaven, I am filled with love at the idea
of You, long ago—long before words and pages,
stories and songs, Adam and Eve—deciding that
You wanted us. That you wanted *me.* This is a
story I want to hear again and again. I cannot
wait until I get to heaven and I can ask You to
tell it to me. When I look at my children, I want
to tell them this story too. I want to tell them
how God loved us even before we were born, just
as I loved them before they were born. Before I
saw their faces. Before I knew their names. What
great love! Amen.

THINK ABOUT IT:
What have you told (or will you tell) your children
about how they entered your family? What have
you told (or will you tell) them about how you
entered God's family?

AS A MOTHER

*"As a mother comforts her child,
so will I comfort you."*

ISAIAH 66:13

A cool palm on a hot forehead. A sweet whisper in the ear of a mind full of hurt feelings. A soft breath blowing on a boo-boo. A generous handful of change when only a quarter was asked for. A word of praise at just the right moment. A beam of pride when a goal is reached. A warm, plush hug when sorrow is heavy. A quiet tear that expresses understanding. A guiding principle when instruction is needed. Lord, You know the ways to comfort us, as well as our own mothers do. You know us even better, and Your comfort is always available. Thank You for that promise. And thank You for moms. Amen.

THINK ABOUT IT:
Think about one way your mom used to comfort you. What did that feel like? How does it feel knowing God will comfort you both now and forever?

GOOD PLANS

The plans of the Lord stand firm forever, the purposes of his heart through all generations.

PSALM 33:11

Lord, I have so many plans for my children. There's so much I want for them. And yet I know there is so much out of my control. What I want most of all is for them to know You and follow You, Lord. I want them to be good people. I want them to be happy, yes, but more than that, I want them to find contentment and joy in You. Help me teach them to do that. Then please help me remember these dreams I have for them as they get older and the time nears for them to make decisions about colleges and careers. Help me not to get too anxious over the process but to remember the goals. Amen.

THINK ABOUT IT:
What hopes and dreams do you have for your children? What hopes and dream do you think God might have for them?

NEARER, NEARER

*Come near to God and he
will come near to you.*

JAMES 4:8

When I am feeling down on myself and a little bit depressed, sometimes I wander away from You, Lord. I don't know why—maybe it's because I know You will remind me of all the goodness in my life, and maybe I'm not ready to hear about that. Or maybe it's because I'm afraid You will be ashamed of my behavior. But, Lord, I know You love me. Just as surely as I would hold out my arms to my own child for a big bear hug, I know You are holding out Your arms to me. Help me to remember to come to You with any problem, big or small. Help me to remember that little eyes are watching me. . .to see where I go for help when trouble comes. Amen.

THINK ABOUT IT:
Who do you turn to when you are feeling low? Where is God on that list?

FORGIVEN MUCH

"Her many sins have been forgiven—
as her great love has shown. But whoever
has been forgiven little loves little."

LUKE 7:47

God, I can't believe I've messed things up yet again. It's just a silly mistake. A stupid misunderstanding. I blame sleep deprivation. But I've really done it, and it's totally my fault. Lord, help me, please. Give me the best words to use to ask for forgiveness. And please help my child to understand. Let this moment be a lesson for both of us. A lesson in forgiveness and grace. A lesson in generosity of spirit, Lord. A lesson in humility for me. Lord God, it seems like I've had a lot of these lessons, doesn't it? I guess I have so much to learn! And I guess I should love a lot more! Amen.

THINK ABOUT IT:
What have you needed to ask forgiveness for lately? How does receiving God's forgiveness feel?

NO PROBLEM

*"With your help I can advance against a troop;
with my God I can scale a wall."*

2 SAMUEL 22:30

Lord, we have a big transition coming up. And there's so much to organize and sort and pack . . .just so much to do. And guess who's been put in charge of all that? Yep, it's me. I suppose I nominated myself, and that's okay. I can do it. But I need my family members to be helpful. And it wouldn't hurt if they were also gracious and, well, would just give me a break every now and then. I'm so glad I can count on Your help always, Lord. Whenever I need a friend, a listening ear, or a wise reply, I know I can come to You. With Your help, I can do anything. I can even pack and move all our belongings in two weeks or less. No problem. Right, Lord? Amen.

THINK ABOUT IT:
What's one big problem that God has helped you with?

HOW ABUNDANT

*How abundant are the good things that
you have stored up for those who fear
you, that you bestow in the sight of all,
on those who take refuge in you.*

PSALM 31:19

Lord of safety, Lord of my security, Lord of refuge,
Lord who saves me—I thank You for the many
times You have kept me from real danger. I pray
that You keep watch over my children as well. I
know You love them more than I ever could, and
You can see any harm in their way far before I
could. God, I don't really know how to thank You
for all that You've already done for my family. I just
know that I need to keep telling people about it. I
want people to hear our stories and trust in You.
And every time I tell our stories, I'm reminded
once again of the abundant blessings You have
poured out on me and my family. Amen.

THINK ABOUT IT:
What good things has God bestowed on you?

WATER CYCLE WONDERS

"How great is God—beyond our understanding!
The number of his years is past finding out. He
draws up the drops of water, which distill as
rain to the streams; the clouds pour down their
moisture and abundant showers fall on mankind."

JOB 36:26-28

Lord, today I was going over the water cycle with my son. And as I watched him coloring a picture that showed how the water is drawn up into the sky, formed into clouds, and then deposited back on the earth, I was amazed at the efficiency and intelligence of the design of these systems You created. They allow us to live, breathe, work, and grow on this earth. I'm so amazed by Your creation, Lord! I'm stunned by the majesty of every detail. You care so much for us. You really did think of everything! Thank You, Lord, for revealing these wonders to my son. Amen.

THINK ABOUT IT:
What is something in nature that amazes you? What facet of God does that reveal?

PROVISIONS

*"He has shown kindness by giving you rain
from heaven and crops in their seasons;
he provides you with plenty of food and
fills your hearts with joy."*

ACTS 14:17

Lord, as I strolled through the grocery aisles today, I was struck by how many choices I have available to me. How fortunate I am, Lord! Some days I feel tightly squished by the confines of our budget—I can't buy everything I want for my children. I can't give them everything their little hearts desire. But they have clean clothes, a safe place to live, and good food every day. I have so many choices, Lord. And today You showed me I can choose to help others too. I can choose to give to others, to be an extension of Your provision. I can choose to rain down loving-kindness and spread Your joy. Amen.

THINK ABOUT IT:
What can you do to help provide for others? What might God be prompting you to share?

TIME IS SHORT

"The grass withers and the flowers fall,
but the word of our God endures forever."

ISAIAH 40:8

Pictures, pictures, pictures. So many photos to sort through—here she is at two. Here he is at three. Here they are on their first bikes. Here's the first tooth in, first tooth lost, first day of braces on, first day of braces off. So many scenes are flashing through my mind as I look at these photos, Lord. And I want to make time stop or just slow down—a lot. I want to remember every moment. Every smile. Every laugh. Every tear. I want to savor it all. Lord, do You ever want us to slow down too? To take a little more time to be together and love each other? Do You ever wish we were paying more attention to each other? We are here for such a short time. Help us to make the most of it. Amen.

THINK ABOUT IT:
What could help you remember to slow down and spend time with your family? With Father God?

LORD OF MY SCHEDULE

*Now listen, you who say, "Today or tomorrow
we will go to this or that city, spend a year there,
carry on business and make money." Why, you do
not even know what will happen tomorrow. What
is your life?. . . Instead, you ought to say, "If it is
the Lord's will, we will live and do this or that."*

JAMES 4:13–15

Wow, God, sometimes I feel like You are talking
directly and solely to me. Have You been checking
out my calendar? Do You see how every day is filled
with one activity after another (and sometimes
two or three on top of each other)? Lord, I know
that sometimes I get caught up in the frenzy of
my family's life. Help me not become imprisoned
by the schedule. Help me to leave space for You,
Lord. No—help me instead to put You first! Amen.

THINK ABOUT IT:
Have you left space on Your calendar for God? If
not, what can you do to schedule Him in?

MY SECRET

*And this is love: that we walk in
obedience to his commands.*

2 JOHN 1:6

God, I have a secret to tell You. You know how I'm always telling my kids they've got to learn to obey? How I'm always going on and on about how important it is to develop a habit of obedience? How we all have to submit to the will of God, even us grown-ups? And how we need to learn to embrace the joy that comes through that obedience? Yeah. Well, I'm not so good at it. I'm guessing You knew that about me already. I'm not good at submitting when I don't understand why. I'm not good at obeying when I want to do something else instead. In fact, I'm just about as difficult as the kids are sometimes, Lord. And I should know better! God, thank You for putting up with me. Please keep teaching me. Amen.

THINK ABOUT IT:

When do you most have trouble obeying God? What Bible verse or story might inspire you to become more obedient?

STAND UP

"Stand up in the presence of the aged, show respect for the elderly and revere your God."

LEVITICUS 19:32

Lord, I am so tired of seeing and hearing children act in ways that are so disrespectful. And sometimes the disrespectful ones are my own children! We live in a culture that doesn't value the elderly as much as it should. Please help me find ways to show my children how important it is to love and honor those who have walked through this life ahead of us. Help me find ways to involve them in the lives of their grandparents and to value the roots from which they have come. And, Lord, please help me to model this respect in the time I give to those who are older, and in my care of and thoughtfulness for them. Lord, help us to stand up and honor every human being. Amen.

THINK ABOUT IT:
How can you show your children how to love and respect the elderly? Who might God be prompting you to reach out to?

CAUSES AND EFFECTS

What causes fights and quarrels among
you? Don't they come from your
desires that battle within you?

JAMES 4:1

Almighty God, I know I am powerless—truly, I have nothing that compares to Your might. So why do I sometimes get so caught up in taking control? I see this in how I interact with my children, and then in how they interact with one another. Sometimes we fight over what seems like nothing at all. But then I take a step back, and I can see I am worried about losing my influence on my children. I can admit that I fear that other voices are having an effect on their minds. I know I've taught them how to make good decisions. But I guess I just wonder if I've taught them well enough. Lord, help me to realize that I really can trust You, and I can trust them. . .at least, with some things. Amen.

THINK ABOUT IT:
What's at the root of your fights and quarrels? In what ways can you invite God into the situation?

OUT OF HIDING

Whoever conceals their sins does not prosper, but the one who confesses and renounces them finds mercy.

PROVERBS 28:13

My Deliverer, I have sinned. I am weighed down by shame. I am troubled by my weakness to temptation, neglect of my duties, and lack of self-control. I am deeply disturbed by things that seem to take over my thoughts. I want to be clean. Yet so often I also just want to hide away—even from You. Help me to find someone trustworthy to confide in. Help me to find people who will keep me accountable and to have the courage to invite them into my life. And help me to come to You even when my strongest desire is to run far away. I don't want these sins to eat away at me and hurt my family. I want to be a strong, good role model for my children, Lord. Please help me. Amen.

THINK ABOUT IT:
What sins do you need to confess? How does it feel knowing God loves you—no matter what?

HUMBLE AND GENTLE

Be completely humble and gentle; be patient,
bearing with one another in love.

EPHESIANS 4:2

I can be humble, Lord. I often have a hard time being proud of myself—though I am always proud of my kids. But gentleness, Lord? That one is a little more difficult. I have learned to be tough—all my life I have worked hard and had to prove myself. I have had difficult things happen to me and have been treated harshly. So sometimes when my child comes to me with hurt feelings or flesh, I am not patient. I tend to want him to just get over it and move on. And I sometimes catch a glimpse of the surprise in his eyes when I am too harsh or speak too quickly. Lord, help me to find the right words to use, to take time, to find the gentleness I know You have placed in me. Amen.

THINK ABOUT IT:
What is most difficult for you—humility, gentleness, or patience? What Bible verse might help you grow in that area?

EARLY MORNINGS

*"Arise, shine, for your light has come,
and the glory of the Lord rises upon you."*

ISAIAH 60:1

Lord of the dawn, I know there is much glory to behold in the pinky-orange glow of the sun as it peeks up over the horizon. But oh, Lord! I am not made for mornings. Or perhaps, just not for this morning. My brain is foggy and my body is slow, Lord. Help me wake up! Help me have the energy and enthusiasm I need to get these kids moving. Help me be a good example with a pleasant attitude, not to mention patience and kindness—even when it's 6:00 a.m. Lord, I'm so thankful You are the God of every hour. There is not a time when I can't come to You. You are an all-day, every day God, and I praise You and thank You for the light. (Even though it is a little too bright at the moment.) Amen.

THINK ABOUT IT:
What's your favorite time of day? Where is God for you in that stretch of time?

ANGEL FACE

*"I tell you that their angels in heaven always
see the face of my Father in heaven."*

MATTHEW 18:10

Eyes that sparkle with the light from the stars.
Little curved ears that hold all my whispers.
Wispy hairs that float at the slightest puff of
air. A button nose that wrinkles and crinkles
in sleep. Beautifully shaped lips—the work of a
master sculptor. Irresistibly soft, plump cheeks
that I cannot stop kissing. This, my little angel
face, is my blessing. My gift from God. How could
anyone not love this face? How will I ever lay this
baby down to sleep? How will my heart survive
this experiment of love? At this very moment,
I can't imagine ever being separated from my
baby love. Jesus said the heavenly angels of our
children look on the face of God. And sometimes,
God, I wonder if this child was sent here to tell
me all about Your love. Thank You, Lord. Amen.

THINK ABOUT IT:
What do you remember about the first time you
saw your child? What did that tell you about God's
love?

BEACH BABES

He leads me beside quiet waters,
he refreshes my soul.

PSALM 23:2-3

Lord, today I am thankful for oceans, and for sand, and for sand castles. I'm thankful for the glow of sunbeams and the reflecting sparkles that dance on the waves. These waters are not so quiet—the waves roar and crash on the rocks. These waters trickle and spit and spray and slosh. But oh! They do refresh my soul, Lord! Thank You for knowing exactly what I need, and thank You for providing a way to rest. I know I can't always come to a beach, but I can always come to You. And sitting in Your presence is as warm as lying in the sun, and as comforting as an old familiar story. I love being here and watching my child discover every seashell and pebble—each time with a look and shout of wonder. Oh Lord, wherever we may be, You refresh us all. Thank You! Amen.

THINK ABOUT IT:
Where is one of your happy places to be with your family? Where is one of your happy places to be alone with God?

LET THEM WORK IT OUT

*Like one who grabs a stray dog by the ears is
someone who rushes into a quarrel not their own.*
PROVERBS 26:17

They're at it again, Lord. How old is sibling
rivalry? I suppose as old as the story of Cain and
Abel, right? I know I should just let them work
it out. But sometimes it's so hard to keep my
nose out of it, God. It's hard for me to not just
fix everything—or at least try. But my kids must
learn that there are better ways of resolving their
troubles and reaching a solution than engaging
in constant bickering that leads nowhere. I know
if I interrupt now, I might grab that "stray dog"—
but it wouldn't be wise. Lord, help me to listen
to Your nudges of wisdom. Help me be patient
enough to wait it out. Amen.

THINK ABOUT IT:
What do you usually do when your children are
quarreling? How can God help you wait it out?

MORE HOPE FOR A FOOL

Do you see someone who speaks in haste?
There is more hope for a fool than for them.
PROVERBS 29:20

When will I finally learn to hold my tongue, Lord?
The words seem to tumble out of my mouth before
I even know they are in my brain. And why is it
that the words that come out the fastest always
seem to be the ones that are the nastiest? Why
can't the nice, pleasant, and kind words come out
first? Never mind. I think I know the answer. Lord,
please, please, *please* help me to slow my mouth
down. Shut me up, Lord. When nasty words are
jumping at the gates, help me to remember that
I want more hope than there is for a fool. I want
to make You proud, Lord. Amen.

THINK ABOUT IT:
When do you have the most trouble holding your
tongue? What scripture can you mentally recite
to help you curb your tongue in such situations?

GOD OF GLORY

The voice of the LORD is over the waters;
the God of glory thunders, the LORD
thunders over the mighty waters.

PSALM 29:3

Lightning flashes across the sky—making the room glow for just a moment. Then with a low rumble, the thunder rolls through the house, rattling the windows. My little one's arms squeeze tight around my neck. The thunder seems so big—too big for us to understand. You are big, Lord. Big and powerful and strong and glorious. I tell my child that sometimes You speak like the thunder—in a voice that rumbles and rages. And sometimes You speak like the spring rain—softly pattering on our paths. But what we can be sure of, and what can calm our fears, is that You always speak. And You are always in control. Thank You, Lord, God of glory, God of thunder. Amen.

THINK ABOUT IT:
What is something in nature that reminds you of a quality of God?

POURED OUT FOR MANY

"This is my blood of the covenant, which is poured out for many for the forgiveness of sins."

MATTHEW 26:28

Father God, I want my children to know about Your Son and all that He did for us. But I'm not sure how to explain to my little ones about how Jesus died. They are scared by the idea of blood. I don't want them to be scared about Jesus too. Help me talk to them in ways they can understand. Help me tell them the whole story—the truth of Jesus' life, death, and resurrection. When the time is right, help me lead them to understand forgiveness, and what Your forgiveness of our sins means. As I do so, Lord, draw my children—and me—ever closer to You. Amen.

THINK ABOUT IT:

What are some ways you can explain the Gospel story to little children?

WALKING IN THE WAY

Follow God's example, therefore, as dearly loved children and walk in the way of love, just as Christ loved us and gave himself up for us as a fragrant offering and sacrifice to God.

Ephesians 5:1-2

I am so relieved, Lord, that You gave us Your Word to follow. And I'm especially glad I'm not the only example my children have of living a good life. For I know I often don't walk very well in the way of love—I don't even walk very well in the way of "like." Sometimes I walk in the way of grumpiness, arrogance, or sarcasm. And other times I walk in the way of anger, bitterness, or folly. I could, in fact, be a great example for my children of where *not* to walk. But, Lord, I want to be better. I want to show my children how they are dearly loved—by You *and* me. Give me the power, strength, and determination to walk in the way of love so I can lead them to the Lord of love, to Christ Himself. Amen.

THINK ABOUT IT:
What does God's "way of love" look like to you? What are some specific ways you can demonstrate this to your children?

TAKING UP THE CROSS

*"Whoever wants to be my disciple
must deny themselves and take up
their cross daily and follow me."*

LUKE 9:23

I wonder, Lord, did You know what my cross would be? I wonder if You knew I would one day be struggling with mounting debt and unmet standards. I wonder if You considered how much I would battle against rule-following, rigid bureaucrats, or tight-lipped, tightly wound authoritarians. I wonder if You knew I would chafe against the ties that were binding me and keep wandering away to find my path. I wonder, Lord, if You knew that every day little hands would remind me to take up my cross yet again and, once on my shoulders, how that cross wouldn't seem so heavy after all. Thank You, Lord, for waiting for me to catch up. And thanks for sharing my load. Amen.

THINK ABOUT IT:
What does your daily cross look like? How does God lighten that load?

WHAT HUMBLE LOOKS LIKE

Humble yourselves before the Lord,
and he will lift you up.

JAMES 4:10

Lord, I don't think of myself as proud, yet I know sometimes I feel pretty satisfied with myself. I don't think of myself highly, yet I don't think I am the lowest of the low. I don't think I know everything, yet I think I know more than almost everyone else in my house—and perhaps even my neighborhood. I can see I've got a long way to go to reach true humility. So I come to You on hands and knees, Lord, and I ask You, please humble me. Show me what true humility looks like. I watch my children and see how they go about in the world with trusting confidence, but not a hint of pride. And I want to be like them. I want to be humbled, so You can lift me up and I, in turn, can lift them up to You. Amen.

THINK ABOUT IT:
Who do you know who reflects humility? Which of that person's traits could you adopt to become more humble yourself?

FROM SACKCLOTH TO JOY

You turned my wailing into dancing; you removed my sackcloth and clothed me with joy, that my heart may sing your praises and not be silent.

PSALM 30:11–12

Singer of my soul, I never thought that one of the benefits of having children would be how much they help me deal with grief. After a loved one has died, it seems impossible to go on with normal life. And yet, my children demand that I do go on with life as normal. They want breakfast; they want stories; they want songs. They will not be silent. And so, Lord, neither shall I. I will sing songs of praise. I will dance. And I will know Your joy. Thank You for letting me grieve, and thank You for providing comfort to me through these beautiful children. Amen.

THINK ABOUT IT:
How have your children helped you process grief or loss? How has God helped?

THE EVILS OF FRETTING

Refrain from anger and turn from wrath;
do not fret—it leads only to evil.

PSALM 37:8

Lord, You know that "Fret" could be my middle name. I tend to act as though I'm at peace, and yet underneath I'm doing it—fretting. And I totally get how it leads to evil. Fretting steals my joy and distracts me from my hope. It takes a good situation and throws a veil of uncertainty over it. Many times I fret over my children—about whether I have clothed, fed, or taught them well enough. Fretting is the devil's game to keep me so occupied with worry and anxiety that I get irritated and angry at everyone around me. Help me not to fret anymore, Lord. Help me break the habit. Amen.

THINK ABOUT IT:
What do you fret about? What scripture might you cling to in order to de-fret?

PROPER RESPECT

Show proper respect to everyone, love the family of believers, fear God, honor the emperor.

1 PETER 2:17

Lord, we are living in such a time when I don't even know if people recognize what proper respect looks like! People openly scoff and speak with contempt about our leaders, and our leaders in turn twist words and devise messages meant to cut others down and sow seeds of discord instead of promoting harmony and peace. God, it is easy to love the family of believers when everyone is getting along well. But when we are all so different, with such varied goals and perspectives, it can get tricky. Lord, help me to talk with people I trust and respect about the best way forward. And in the meantime, help me start with the basics with my children—to teach them to honor their mother and father. Amen.

THINK ABOUT IT:
Do you know someone who speaks with respect toward others, no matter who they are? What might God want you to learn from him or her?

LIKE WAX

*The mountains melt like wax before the
LORD, before the Lord of all the earth.
The heavens proclaim his righteousness,
and all peoples see his glory.*

PSALM 97:5-6

God of glory, I see Your hugeness, the enormity
of Your strength, and the might of Your hand. I
know You are bigger than the mountains and
fiercer than the molten core of this planet. You
are to be feared. Lord, help me show my child
that the God we serve is bigger, better, stronger,
wiser, and more full of love for us than any other
god that people may claim. As my little one and
I lie on our backs and gaze at the heavens, let
the massiveness of Your creation fill my child's
mind with awe. Let Your creativity dazzle my
child's young thoughts. Amen.

THINK ABOUT IT:
What leads you to be filled with awe of God?

NO MORE FIGHTING

If it is possible, as far as it depends
on you, live at peace with everyone.

ROMANS 12:18

I feel as if I need to embroider the verse above
on a blanket, then hang it up in every room. And
the message is not just for my children, but for
me. God, You know how I have a habit of pushing
buttons. Sometimes I can't just leave the little
things alone—I have to pick out something
negative to say. And it inevitably leads to trouble.
Then I see my children following my example.
They pick at each other when they should be
playing. God, I know that not everything is in
my hands, but as far as it is in my power to do
so, please help me find ways to live at peace with
every person in my house, on my street, in my
community, and in this world. Amen.

THINK ABOUT IT:
What's stopping you from living at peace with
others? What Bible verses might help you become
more of a peace-maker than a peace-taker?

BABY STEPS

The LORD makes firm the steps of the one who delights in him; though he may stumble, he will not fall, for the LORD upholds him with his hand.

PSALM 37:23-24

The chunky little toes grab and stretch, providing balance for the toddler who is depending on them so wholeheartedly. The child's eyes fixate on the toy he wants. He wavers a little as he stands, looking and longing. Then a chubby hand reaches out, fingers spread wide. The dimpled knee bends, the sole of the foot lifts off from the floor and comes down again with a thump. And there it is—one step. A small step for this little man, but a giant leap for his parents. Lord, help us to rejoice in these moments together. As we watch these first steps, please remind us that You are with us every step of our lives. Amen.

THINK ABOUT IT:

What "first" moments have you enjoyed lately? How does it feel knowing you've got God's support every first, every second?

ACCEPT ONE ANOTHER

Accept one another, then, just as Christ accepted you, in order to bring praise to God.

ROMANS 15:7

Lord, I watch my children sometimes, not to see whether they have been listening to me but because I need to learn from them. They so easily approach those who are different from them. They play with anyone—no one is a stranger. They find out people's names and learn what they like to do. They give hugs at the drop of a hat. They get excited over the smallest of victories. They rejoice together. And if someone is sad, they try to find out what's wrong and fix it right away. Lord, I want to be like my children. I want to be like You. Please help me accept others as Jesus did. I praise You, Father. Amen.

THINK ABOUT IT:
What lessons has God been teaching you through your children lately?

REMEMBER THOSE

Continue to remember those in prison as if you were together with them in prison, and those who are mistreated as if you yourselves were suffering.

HEBREWS 13:3

Lord, it would be awfully easy for me to put my children in a bubble and keep them there until they are eighteen. I want to shield them from the darker side of life. Yet I know that they should not feel afraid of people who are stumbling on this life journey, Lord. Everyone makes mistakes. Everyone makes bad choices. We are all the same on the inside—just human beings trying to figure out how to live life. Help me to remind my children that crime isn't catching and that suffering doesn't rub off if you get too close to a person. Help me to show them that when we care for those who are stuck in prison or in suffering, we help to bring them freedom, and that by loving others, we show people what it means to love God. Amen.

THINK ABOUT IT:
What is God nudging you to do to remember those who have been removed from our sight?

THE TRUTH

"When he, the Spirit of truth, comes,
he will guide you into all the truth."

JOHN 16:13

Lord, I'm worried. I have tried to teach my children to be truthful and to seek truth in all things. However, I know there are many sophisticated companies out there, crafting messages that are designed to manipulate facts and manufacture their own version of truth. And I know no matter how much I train my children, they will be exposed to these confusing images and tales. Lord, help me keep my ears tuned to the sound of Your wisdom. Help me motivate my children to practice looking for the truth so they know it when they see or hear it. Help me guide them to the right paths. Amen.

THINK ABOUT IT:
Think about a time in the past when you had a hard time deciphering truth from fiction. How can God help you discern the truth in the future?

INTO THE WORLD

*This is how God showed his love among us:
He sent his one and only Son into the
world that we might live through him.*

1 JOHN 4:9

I can't get over what You did for us, Lord. As a mom, I can't fathom giving my children up—even for people I love. And the idea of giving up my son or daughter for people who don't even deserve it? Unfathomable. Yet You did just that for us. For me. You did that so we could have a chance to live with You in heaven for eternity. And if I spend every minute from now until I see You in heaven, telling You how grateful I am for that sacrifice, it will never be enough. Lord, thank You, thank You, thank You. Amen.

THINK ABOUT IT:
What is one way you can show your thanks to God this week?

ROOTED

"My eyes will watch over them for their good, and I will bring them back to this land. I will build them up and not tear them down; I will plant them and not uproot them."

JEREMIAH 24:6

Lord, You've seen me working in my garden. You know I have a hard time deciding what plants are flowers and which are weeds. I try not to tear down the good and lovely plants with the strangling, wild ones. I want the flowers to grow and be strong. So I do try to uproot and remove those pesky weeds. God, when I look at the garden of my children, I ask You to help me keep them planted in good soil, water them frequently, and help them to grow tall and bold for You. Help me to dig down deep with my own roots so that I have a strong foundation my seedlings can lean on. Amen.

THINK ABOUT IT:
How do you stay rooted in your faith? What Bible verse has been watering your spirit lately?

A PURE HEART

Create in me a pure heart, O God,
and renew a steadfast spirit within me.
PSALM 51:10

Lord, I get weighed down by the list of sins that seems to grow every day. I know You don't keep a record of wrongs. I know that once You have forgiven me, I am indeed forgiven. But Lord, I keep falling back into my old ways. I keep losing my patience. I keep saying harsh words to my children. I keep relying on deception instead of just holding on to the truth. Lord, please make my heart pure. Make my desires be like Yours. Make my spirit strong and constant so I can stick to Your plan for me and my family. I know I am responsible for teaching my children Your ways. Help me, Lord, to live up to all You ask of me. Amen.

THINK ABOUT IT:
What will it take for your heart to be pure today? What words of God can help renew your spirit?

TEACHINGS WE FORGET

*Listen, my son, to your father's instruction
and do not forsake your mother's teaching.*

PROVERBS 1:8

God, I know I should thank her. I know I should let my mother know how many times she has been right. But it's hard to admit it, Lord. So hard! I want to go my own way, make my own mistakes, take my own steps. But her voice is in my head—trying to tell me what to do and how to do it. The thing is, even when I didn't want to, I learned so much from her. I learned from the words she taught me and the things she showed me how to do. And I learned when she wasn't even noticing—just by watching her. Lord, I know my child is watching me now. God, help me not to mess this up! Amen.

THINK ABOUT IT:
What did you learn from your mother? What are you still learning from her voice in your head? What are you learning from God's voice?

NURSING

Just as a nursing mother cares for her children,
so we cared for you. Because we loved you so
much, we were delighted to share with you not
only the gospel of God but our lives as well.

1 THESSALONIANS 2:7–8

The beautiful thing about nursing is not just the act itself, but it is in what the mother gives besides milk from her body. The milk is the symbol of all the many small and large sacrifices to come. Sacrifices of time and money, of energy and will, of gifts and achievements. Lord, let me remember this act of love as a symbol of how we are to feed and care for others—not just providing the facts or the Gospel message, but giving from our hearts as well. When we share our lives with others, we show them what living in Your kingdom is really like. Please open up my heart to share my life with Your children, Lord. Amen.

THINK ABOUT IT:
In what ways can you share your life—and the Gospel—with others?

IN HIS HAND

*"In his hand is the life of every creature
and the breath of all mankind."*

JOB 12:10

Lord, as I sit here holding my child, watching the rise and fall of her chest as she breathes, I think about how precious she is. I can't imagine her breath ever stopping without mine stopping too. And I think about how fragile we are. There are so many things that can go wrong with our bodies, so many diseases that can hurt us, and accidents that can harm us. Lord, I rest here knowing that my child and I are in Your hands—and that makes me feel both very small and very safe. I know You, who gave us breath, will not take it away on a whim. I know You, who created the world with Your words and formed us with Your hands, will take very good care of every one of Your masterpieces. I trust You, Lord. Amen.

THINK ABOUT IT:
What does it feel like to be held in God's hands?

LITTLE CHILDREN

*"Let the little children come to me,
and do not hinder them, for the kingdom
of God belongs to such as these."*

MARK 10:14

Lord, help me to remember—when my life is busy,
my work demanding, and people at every turn
asking me for help—that I can learn from my
children. I can slow down. I can focus intently on
one tiny thing at a time. I can laugh easily. I can
love with a big heart and big hugs. I can smile
at everyone I see. I can dance with abandon. I
can run barefoot. I can sing loud. I can make up
stories. I can sit and listen too. I can be Your child,
Lord. I can come to You. Now and forever. Amen.

THINK ABOUT IT:
Imagine you are one of the children in the crowd,
coming to see Jesus. What would you like to
ask Him?

SCRIPTURE INDEX

IF YOU LIKED THIS BOOK,
YOU'LL WANT TO TAKE A LOOK AT. . .

3-MINUTE DEVOTIONS
FOR THE WORKPLACE

3-Minute Devotions for the Workplace includes more than 180 readings that address the real-life issues of employment—integrity, office politics, coworker relations, and more—that can be read in 3 minutes! Written primarily for the office worker, this devotional will encourage you to rely on God's underlying plan for your life.

Paperback / 978-1-68322-237-8 / $4.99